BU

AND
SELLING A
BUSINESS

WITHDRAWN
FROM STOCK

BUYING AND SELLING A BUSINESS

An Entrepreneur's Guide

JO HAIGH

PIATKUS

❧❧ *Visit the Piatkus website!*

Piatkus publishes a wide range of bestselling fiction and non-fiction, including books on health, mind, body & spirit, sex, self-help, cookery, biography and the paranormal.

If you want to:
- read descriptions of our popular titles
- buy our books over the internet
- take advantage of our special offers
- enter our monthly competition
- learn more about your favourite Piatkus authors

VISIT OUR WEBSITE AT: **www.piatkus.co.uk**

Copyright © 2007 by Jo Haigh

First published in 2007 by
Piatkus Books Limited
5 Windmill Street
London WIT 2JA
e-mail: info@piatkus.co.uk

The moral right of the author has been asserted

A catalogue record for this book is available from the British Library

ISBN 0 7499 2739 9
ISBN 13 978 0 7499 2739 4

Edited Andy Armitage
Design and typestting by Paul Saunders

This book has been printed on paper manufactured with respect for the environment using wood from managed sustainable resources

Printed and bound in Great Britain by
William Clowes Ltd, Beccles, Suffolk

To Bongo, the best sister in the world.

Entrepreneur defined

'A calculated risk taker'
JO HAIGH

'A calculating risk taker'
EDWARD CLIFFORD chair, Vistage International

Contents

Part 3 Selling

Acknowledgements

As always these things are never a lone exercise.

Without my wonderful PA, Natalie Fisher, it would simply be impossible to write a book and do my day job. Natalie, relentless patience is simply unquantifiable.

I would also like to say a special thanks to Karen Farrington and Albert DePetrillo for their invaluable help and encouragement, which enabled me to complete this book and keep it user-friendly!

I would also like to thank GNER for their constant supply of teas and coffees on the innumerable journeys where much of this book was written, along with my fabulous hairdresser – yes, hairdresser! – Jeannette, who always found me a quiet corner in which to rewrite the various sections as she patiently tried to cut my unkempt locks!

Foreword

IN MY CAREER IN THE media, my work with YFM Group and my
many and varied connections with public-sector agencies it
has always been clear to me that everything has a value but that
different people price that value in different ways and levels.
Whether it is a new TV series, a company that is for sale, some
interesting intellectual property, an industrial estate or a public
service, it has financial worth.

In a market economy, entrepreneurs are always looking for
undervalued assets that they can exploit for profit. In the public sector our brightest minds are looking to develop those
services that offer the best returns in terms of end user benefits
and cost-effective delivery.

Buying and selling businesses and assets – and coming to a
view about the value of those businesses and assets – has been a
critically important part of my life. So, I particularly welcome
this, Jo Haigh's latest book, as a good, practical read for those
entrepreneurs and decision makers who want to seek out fresh
opportunities and to add value for the benefit of their customers
and their shareholders or employers.

SIR CLIVE LEACH CBE, chairman of YFM Group *

---

* Clive Leach is the former chairman and chief executive of Yorkshire Tyne Tees
Television. After a successful career in the media, Clive has held a number of
top level posts in the skills-development, training and cultural industry sectors in
the Yorkshire and Humber region. He is executive chairman of the venture-
capital and consulting-services company, the YFM Group, the UK's most active
investor in small and medium-sized enterprises.

A LITTLE LEARNING, it is said, can be a dangerous thing. But, when it comes to buying or selling a business, the more you know about the process, the risks and the pitfalls, the better prepared you will be to handle them.

For most people, the acquisition or sale of a business is a once-in-a-lifetime event. Reading this book is not intended to make you an expert on the subject, but it will help you to assess what specialists you may need during the process, what role they will play and, importantly, what you should expect from them to achieve the best results.

The laws, rules and regulations surrounding sale and purchase of businesses are extensive and often complex. Getting it wrong can have serious consequences. This book gives an outline of some of the issues with which you will need to grapple. Part of the key to success is not necessarily knowing the answer to a problem, but realising there is a difficulty that needs dealing with in the first place. The author has addressed this with a straightforward approach to the key issues you may face, without seeking to baffle you with jargon.

One of the key messages of the book is the need to surround yourself with good and trusted advisers. Running a business is often a lonely affair and the pressure of a major event, such as selling the business you have built up over the years, should never be underestimated. A good adviser will be one who gives you the counsel you need to deal with the complexities of the deal, whether legal or financial. A top-notch adviser is one who does that and more – providing you with a sounding board, listening to you, giving you an unbiased and commercially sound viewpoint and helping to ease the pressure. They should help you to take the heat out of what can often be difficult negotiations and maintain focus and momentum throughout. Take time choosing the team you will work with; you will spend many hours with them, so you need both to feel confident in them and to get on with them.

In reading this book, you have taken the most important step in the process of buying or selling a business – planning.

Understanding why you wish (or need) to sell or buy a business is fundamental to achieving your aims. It will dictate much of the activity that follows. I wish you every success.

CARL CHAMBERS, CFO, Spice Holdings PLC *

---

* Carl is a chartered accountant having qualified with Deloitte Haskins & Sells in 1988. He then pursued a career in corporate finance and mergers and acquisitions. Following a period with 3i, he held a number of top level posts at NatWest, Midland Bank and Coutts Bank. During his time with the Spice Holdings Group, Carl has had the roles of chief executive of team telecom and chief financial officer, before becoming corporate development director in May 2005.

Introduction

'Many an optimist became rich by buying out a pessimist'

– ROBERT G. ALLEN

G ENERALLY, MOST PEOPLE buy or sell a business only once in a lifetime. For many it is the realisation of a dearly held dream. The journey to purchase or sell is fraught with thrills and spills. It's like skiing a black run in Val d'Isère having put on skis only for the first time that morning!

This book is aimed at those of us who want to turn dreams into reality, to be our own boss or to convert years of hard toil into a comfortable and satisfying financial return. Typically, readers will have an aversion to lawyers and accountants, in particular to their fees! But there's recognition, too, that they would benefit from professional expertise. They will know they are novices in achieving their current aspirations, be it an acquisition or disposal, but are driven and sufficiently ambitious to explore their ultimate goals.

This book is aimed at entrepreneurs in the making with a desire for enlightenment among the mayhem of mergers and acquisitions, which we will term corporate finance. It will take you through the whole process of a 'would-be' transaction. In relation to an acquisition it will cover:

- identification of targets;

- the dating and mating process;

- agreeing the terms of the transaction;

- finding and keeping the right finance;

- making it work.

And, for disposals, the book will cover:

- pre-grooming:
  - the business
  - the people
  - the finances;

- finding the buyers;

- structuring a deal;

- ensuring a clean and worry-free final exit;

- maximising the value and security of the deal.

Each section will provide essential guidance on the legal and financial minefields attached to any transaction and will ensure you are fully aware of the critical issues that need addressing correctly in the first place, to ensure as stress-free a deal as possible.

Terminology used in corporate finance can be relentlessly intimidating, leaving the uninitiated vulnerable and exposed. This book will explain the most frequently used terms, providing the entrepreneur with essential insight into the mysteries of the process.

PART 1

Groundwork

CHAPTER 1

To Begin at the Beginning

THIS BOOK CONTAINS masses of advice on specific questions, but assumes you have started, or are ready to start, the process. However, I suggest you ask yourself and your support teams some pertinent questions before starting on the roller-coaster ride.

An existing business versus a startup – the pros and cons

For the novice entrepreneur, starting a business from scratch would seem to be most logical thing to do. After all, you can choose where to base it, what it will sell, whom you will sell to and where you will buy from. In addition, you can set up your own systems and select your personal advisers. In fact, you could become a regular megalomaniac!

With modest expectations you might not need lots of funding. You might even be able to access grants unavailable to existing companies. Given the number of serviced offices or short-term licensed premises at hand, the risks and costs can be very limited and, best of all, you will achieve the ultimate satisfaction of creating something from nothing.

The disadvantages are somewhat more far-reaching. Success

requires a good idea with potential to exploit the market or enter new markets. Do you have that? Bear in mind that three quarters of all startups fail in the first year. A quarter of those that succeed in the initial 12 months flounder in the second year, due to lack of knowledge and understanding of the market and also an absence of basic working capital.

Holidays and sick days become a thing of the past. If you start up a new company, working a seven-day week is not at all uncommon. You will need to create a customer base and persuade suppliers to sell to you on credit terms – not easy if you have no performance history and no security to offer. Further, you may have to provide personal guarantees to funders, so, if you fail in your enterprise, personal assets – possibly your home – will have to be realised to settle debts.

While never risk-free, buying an existing business has many advantages over the startup. Provided you purchase at the right price, the risk of failure is much smaller. You have an established market even if it's been underexploited. You will have a customer base and credit lines with suppliers. True, none of these may be ideal, but they are a starting point and, provided you have bought wisely, you will at least have an insight into the potential and be off to a running start.

When you purchase a business it is quite possible that there will be neglected areas in the organisation that will allow you better access to finance. With an ongoing, established customer base, you will have an income stream to service this debt.

If the business you buy is a franchise (and we will look at those later) the failure rate is very low indeed – less than 5 per cent, according to the British Franchise Association (BFA). Costs tend to be lower due to bulk purchasing power and the parent company can provide the business support you need as a franchisee. However, as with any business venture, there are partial drawbacks.

So many business values are linked to the owner of a business that, when your vendor exits stage left, you could find that a large proportion of the value of the business leaves with them. When you buy it is not only visible assets you purchase but also intangible assets (goodwill). Valuing these is an art form, but, whatever you pay, it may end up not looking to be worth quite what it was when you first agreed the deal.

Don't forget that you also take over all employees under the Transfer of Undertaking Protection of Employment Right Act, known as TUPE regulations. This means that all rights, obligations and history pass to you as the new owner, regardless of whether they are essential to you or not. You are stuck with them until you manage them out legally or pay redundancy costs.

Finally, if you are actively looking to buy a business as a management buy-in candidate, (see Chapter 2), you will find that this is a very long and expensive process. If you are not working elsewhere you will not be earning, so remember that 90 per cent of acquirers never do the deal – and those who do never end up buying the business they initially enquired about.

TIMING

The shortest deal I have ever done involved a software business. It had already been approached and courted by a third party and together we sewed up the whole deal in eight weeks. This is extremely unusual. It was a case of buying licences that were very clearly documented. I was acting for vendors, and the acquirers obligingly made an offer that was within a few thousand of the asking price. Deals usually take on average 6–12 months.

The most protracted deal I have been involved with took three and a half years. It concerned the sale of a company in Eire, and the acquirer was a division of a public company. In that time there were two changes of chief executive and on both occasions the deal had to go back to the credit committee to be reviewed. By the end, it was an entirely different deal from the one we started.

Questions for acquirers

Do you have a clear criterion on what you want and where?

Although this may be very broad, some thought must be put into it, if only to narrow down your search. There are thousands of organisations for sale at any one time, although lots, of course, are unsaleable! There are also many businesses that aren't proactively for sale but could be if the right deal were offered.

How much do you really want this?

I don't mean just the end result here – the ownership of the organisation – but also whether you are prepared to put a good part of your life on hold while you embark on a process that is hugely time consuming and highly emotional, not to mention expensive – and may eventually come to nothing.

Have you got the resources to make this work?

This includes personal stamina – trust me, this will be unlike anything you have experienced before. If you think you are working hard now, try running a deal and doing the day job. Lots of meetings will take place out of standard office hours and could, by virtue of the location, involve long periods spent travelling.

Have you got the right internal team around you?

Your mind will inevitably be on the transaction. This means that, as you may neglect your own business, you need to ensure you have delegated some, if not all, of the critical bits of the day job.

Have you got a first-class external professional team?

There is lots more information about buying and selling in this book, but please don't assume you can carry a deal without external help. Unless it is an extremely modest transaction, it's unlikely to happen. Choose advisers who are experienced and make your selection not on price but on quality. Advisers should display a genuine desire to help you succeed. I have seen far too many disastrous transactions where advisers have been appointed because they are cheap or, worse still, because they are friends, regardless of the fact that they have no relevant experience.

Would you ask your GP to carry out a heart bypass? Well, I certainly hope not, so don't choose your auditor as your adviser on a transaction, because that's not what auditors do!

Have you got the backing of your family?

Yes, even those not directly involved in the deal will almost certainly be very much part of the process. My advice is to inform them of your plans and advise them about possible time commitments. You may think it preferable to keep your home as a 'quiet haven'. The truth is, the emotional corkscrew of a deal can be helped along if you have the proactive support of your nearest and dearest.

Are your funders supporting you?

Although you don't always need your own money to carry through a transaction, that may not remain so in the medium and longer term. Although additional cash may not be needed immediately, your funds may well be affected as you progress through the changes of a deal.

My advice is always to keep funders in the picture. Deals have a habit of changing shape and you may need to access funding reserves sooner than you thought. Getting these people on board, if only in principle, earlier rather than later can only be a good thing.

Before you begin your hunt, categorise what it is exactly you are looking for in your ideal target business. Is it

- client lists;

- know-how;

- management or staff skills;

- sites and equipment;

- brands and goodwill?

Think about the size of the organisation, its location and whether or not you are prepared to take on 'basket cases' (a declining business or even a failed one). Draw up your must-haves and your wish list – this will help you, and ultimately your advisers, focus on the right deal for you.

A QUESTION OF VALUE

One of the major stumbling blocks in any transaction, unsurprisingly, is the value of the business concerned. Without hesitation I can say there has never been an acquisition proposed in which the buyer thinks the business is worth more than the vendor's ideal value.

Ultimately, for a transaction to succeed there is inevitably going to be some compromise required from both parties.

How long do you think the deal will take to pull off? Let me assure you, it will take twice as long and cost twice as much as you expect! So, managing expectations among vendors and acquirers is critical for keeping both time and fees in check.

One way of accelerating the process as an acquirer is to look at the deal in the first instance through the eyes of the vendor. Take a realistic view of what you would sell at and under what conditions (Chapter 7 has some advice), using sound commercial sense. Use your findings as guidelines to define the position you are prepared to take in the transaction.

▶

I promise this will improve your chances of building rapport in a transaction and increase your chances of success.

You will also want to take a view on what you are actually buying – or selling (again, see Chapter 7 on structuring the deal). Is it assets and goodwill, or is it shares? Both have different implications for the teams on both sides, not least of which are tax and the cost implications attached to it.

All these issues, if not properly considered, have a nasty habit of causing, at best, an expensive, protracted transaction and, at worst, a lost deal.

Here's a tip. If you are buying, always start the negotiation by asking the other side how much they want for the business. On the other hand, if you are selling, *never tell them!*

Questions for vendors

In addition to the relevance of some of the above questions, and the technical points covered later in this book, here are some other issues for vendors to think about.

Why are you selling?

The answer may well seem quite obvious. Maybe you are in ill health; possibly you want to realise your investment; you may even be considering retirement – but that's not the real question. This cautionary enquiry requires much more profound thought, particularly if you are an owner-manager, and a hands-on one at that.

What will you do when the sale goes through? Dreams of the lotus-eating life are often left unfulfilled, even for those lucky enough to bank large amounts. Mostly this is because many owner-managers have devoted a large proportion of their time to their venture. They have, in all likelihood, either neglected their family and friends or lost them altogether. Therefore, although the financial security may be attractive, the sale may leave them emotionally and practically bereft.

While retirement can be a joy, it may turn out that one day yawns into the next when a once-busy brain lies idle. Make sure you are ready for what lies ahead.

Is your organisation ready to sell?

Is it in the best possible shape? Are your people, products and premises as presentable as possible and likely to attract the most interest?

Just what are you selling?

Other than the assets-versus-shares issue, think branding, history, reputation. Think lifestyle validation and emotional attachments. I have seen vendors cry when the final signature at completion takes place and the new owners make irrevocable changes.

Can you work, and get on, with the new owners?

Sometimes, to maximise value, there is a requirement for vendors to remain with the organisation for varying periods of time. The trouble with this is that it involves your working for someone else in what was once your own company and that is usually extremely difficult.

I have a motto that rarely fails: 'Sell out and get out!' So, if you are intending to continue working with the company after its sale, beware of the pitfalls, especially if additional consideration is linked to your stay.

Have I taken the best possible advice?

Completing the deal may seem like the end. However, it may be just the beginning. As a vendor, you will have made all sorts of promises and commitments about your business. How you provide these is a very important element in retaining your consideration. You will also need the best possible tax and investment advice.

Choose an adviser who is a great negotiator and who flags up commercial risks. Ensure you have a creative tax adviser. These choices made wisely at the start of the process will help you feel more comfortable with the outcome.

Are you ready for a rocky ride?

There will be major ups and downs – lots and lots of downs! Selling a business is not unlike selling a home, since often you will come across time wasters and the financially incapable. Altogether, it's a demanding task that's not for the faint-hearted.

Don't be drinking that champagne when you get your first offer, because, as they say, 'It ain't done until it's done.'

The upsides and downsides of ownership

Owning a business suits some people better than others. By and large, in my experience, it is those who are very driven and ambitious who usually want to make something happen for themselves. In fact 128,000 new businesses were launched in 2005 and VAT registrations were up by more than 10 per cent. So there are plenty of people out there who fit the bill. While it's not the only motive, making money that exceeds an annual salary is often high on the list. Certainly, my advice is that, other than for a few notable exceptions, the only way to make serious money is to run your own successful business!

Everyone at some time in their working life has a desire to 'be the boss', but for many the monthly salary is difficult to forgo. Sometimes the move into self-employment has been forced by redundancy or even dismissal. Maybe it's a chosen path but, whatever the route, the ultimate destination is rarely as expected.

In truth, nothing about ownership is black and white, as

every owner-manager will tell you. Like most things, it has advantages and disadvantages, but there are some areas that are perhaps more significant than others.

- It's likely you will never have worked so hard in your entire life. Knowing that your own livelihood and possibly those of several others depends on your performance tends to concentrate the mind.

- You will have less time for yourself and your family than ever before, although you may be more flexible. One of the reasons I started my own company was the frustration of not attending the children's various school events. Once I had my own company and was effectively the boss I didn't necessarily have the time but I had the choice. I simply moved my working life around the hours I had available.

- If things don't go according to plan, you will be the one who suffers financially. When I had my own company, there were many occasions when I simply couldn't draw a salary, since there weren't enough funds in the bank. Since this was not an idea that would have been welcomed by my staff, I had to take last place in the wages queue.

- You may have to take on guarantees for very substantial debts. Often, with new ventures or even growing ones, the shareholder-directors may have to provide guarantees to funders that allow the business access to finance. If the venture fails, you may be in the unfortunate position of having to cash in assets (often your home) to pay these funders back!

- You will have plenty of sleepless nights. One of the advantages of working for someone else is that, by and large, you can sever work from your home life. As an owner-manager you can never do that, as you and the business are inextricably linked.

- Menial multitasking will become a way of life! Owner-mangers must be prepared to do it all at some point in the business cycle but especially so in the early days and when times get tough. If you have come out of corporate life as top dog, get used to the change – and fast. My husband joined me from an international organisation where he had been managing director. It took him a long while to realise that he was the only person who would do his filing for him. Only when his paperwork reached mountainous levels did a dreadful foreboding of the inevitable finally reach him.

- Running a business feels like having a child. You will have a great sense of achievement and, at other times, a huge amount of frustration. You will have to nurture this offspring, feed and love it. And sometimes the rewards will be minimal. However, as it grows and develops, you will be filled with pride until ultimately you have to let it go, hopefully via a successful sale!

- If you are successful you can make a lot of money. Of course, this may not be your major driving force but it is certainly a pleasant outcome for many people, although by no means a certainty.

- You will have a great sense of satisfaction. Like many owner-managers, I am very proud of what I have achieved and I enjoy seeing the fruits of my labour – not just the material assets, either, but also the wellbeing of my staff and colleagues.

If you are in any way put off embarking on an acquisition hunt by what you have read so far, it's time to shelve the dream of being your own boss. Go for the safer option of the monthly salary in the knowledge that you have lost nothing when, without reading this book, you could have lost everything.

If you still feel that bubbling enthusiasm for adventure and uncertainty – read on.

CHAPTER 2

Who's Who?

THERE WILL ALWAYS BE MANY participants involved in a transaction. Even a fairly simple deal will require legal input of some sort and the more complex the transaction the more people accumulate.

Some are essential, some desirable and some just a luxury, but all these personnel are going to cost money, perhaps a lot more than you first envisaged.

The buyer, purchaser or acquirer

These are interchangeable terms, all meaning largely the same. The nature of this particular beast is, however, a variable one. It could be an individual (you, even). If you are buying into a business you may be known as the management candidate who is participating in a management buy-in (MBI).

Lots of people find the idea of buying into an existing business very appealing: after all, it may offer a ready-made market, brand, product and, for a more substantial business, a management team and infrastructure. However, except for very modest transactions, MBIs are notoriously difficult to complete. They are fraught with problems, not least being the lack of sufficient funds from individuals to invest personally.

Even when the issue can be resolved with, say, the help of third-party funding, a major concern for both the funder and the vendor is the reliance of the deal's success on one person. What happens if that person doesn't perform, becomes too ill to work or, worst-case scenario, dies?

These factors, linked with the possibility that a deal may be done more quickly and far more easily if the business is sold to a trade acquirer, reduce the management candidate's chances of success.

It is possible, however, to turn that around by converting your MBI into a buy-in/management buy-out (BIMBO). This means that both existing management and new managers are involved.

BIMBOs are much more significant players and the chances of completing a transaction successfully are about 100 per cent higher than with the MBI process! The rationale is simple. Funders feel far more secure as the risk is spread across a number of people, both financially and practically. The further injection of new skills, knowledge and finance into an existing management buy-out team (MBO) is yet a further attractive dimension.

Overall, BIMBOs are more likely to complete and succeed in the longer term than either an MBI or an MBO.

WHY AN MBO?

An MBO team is an attractive option, especially when there are external shareholders (that is, shareholders who are not executive directors) who are wishing to sell. Effectively, it's a case of simply transferring ownership onto an established management team (with a proven record) so banks and other funders tend to take a generous view of funding capacity.

A critical factor in an MBO team's success scale is the breadth and robustness of the team. Before moving forward, check that the team is complete. Are there vacancies for the relevant

▶

senior positions across the board, for example, in finance, operations, sales and technical areas? Is there a leader, including a managing director (MD) or chief executive officer (CEO)?

Although some gaps may be justifiably filled by senior management, it is unlikely that a team without an MD or a finance director (FD) will be looked on as favourably as one that has these two senior positions as possible shareholder-directors.

Other potential acquirers can come in the form of institutional investors. These may be private equity houses or more traditional venture capitalists. These types of investor tend to be involved in more substantial deals.

The main difference between these buyers and those previously mentioned is that they rarely bring any practical day-to-day management input to the table. They are essentially funders who place equity in the transaction as opposed to debt, or sometimes as well as debt. As such, they are clearly looking at deals from a different perspective from that of the management team acquirers.

Fundamentally, the main difference is that they want to see a viable exit opportunity, usually within a maximum of five years. In addition, as they are clearly not going to run the business on a day-to-day basis, they need to be pretty comfortable that, when the vendors make their exit, high-calibre personnel are in place to continue running the business. Usually, deals are structured in such a way as to allow the executive management team to participate in the ownership, but not always.

For more modest deals, individuals can buy into companies under the umbrella of the investment of a business angel. Whereas institutional investors talk in millions of pounds, angels tend to talk in terms of thousands. An angel investment can allow a vendor to release some corporate worth either to themselves or to the company – but don't necessarily expect the angel to take part in the management, although this may be a viable option and would need exploring.

Another option for the entrepreneur to explore in terms of possible buying parties is the trade buyer. The trade buyer could be, and often is, a direct competitor, usually, but not always, larger than the vendor. When the acquirer is smaller this is known as a reverse acquisition. He may not be a direct competitor but may see synergies within the market that are ripe for exploitation if the two were to become one, so to speak.

Either way, the problem from the vendor's point of view is the risk associated with leaking vital business information to others who could be on what we might technically term 'a fishing trip', having no real interest in carrying out a deal. Although processes can be undertaken to minimise this in the form of a nondisclosure agreement, these are by no means foolproof.

THE TRADE BUYER

The nature of the trade buyer is worthy of consideration. The listed-company buyer (that is, the buyer of a PLC) will be a very different animal to deal with from, for example, the acquirer of a family-business trade. Both will have merits and their fair share of complications.

PLC buyers tend to take longer to make the decision, due to city controls, budgets and so forth, but usually have far greater access to cash reserves. Conversely, family businesses may be able to make a quicker decision, but access to funding may be problematic.

There are also potential buyers among the general public. There are minor shareholders in listed companies, that is, those listed to trade on the London Stock Exchange (LSE), the Alternative Investment Market (AIM, also part of the LSE), or what is effectively a third market for much smaller companies, Ofex (standing for off exchange). All these markets allow the free buying and selling of shares in the public domain.

▶

Buyers can be what may be termed 'Ma and Pa' buyers – that is, individuals or groups of individuals who hold very small minority investments in one company or more – or they may be large institutional investors.

The latter are generally available only to listed businesses. Although technically there is nothing to stop you offering shares in your company to anyone, you can't deal in such shares in the same way as you can in PLC shares. For instance, in PLCs if you are a director of the company you need to be very careful about your own personal restrictions on selling and buying shares in certain periods of the year. This is due to restrictions by the Financial Services Authority (FSA) on insider dealing, that is, dealing in shares while you're in possession of confidential knowledge about the future welfare of a business.

The seller (or vendor)

Like the buyers, these come in different shapes and sizes. Primarily, the difference between the vendor and the acquirer (apart from being on opposite sides of the transaction) is that the vendor tends to play his cards rather closer to his chest than the buyer, particularly in the early stages. That is not meant to be a criticism; indeed it's entirely acceptable and understandable.

Vendors are naturally cautious of sensitive information about their business spilling into the public domain or, worse still, into their competitors' hands. Especially in owner-managed organisations, there tend to be huge emotional attachments to the business, with which an acquirer is unlikely to empathise.

Clearly, it is far easier to deal with one vendor who has the final say in a transaction. But where the vendor must take into account the views of fellow shareholders or funders, the decision-making process inevitably becomes protracted – and for protracted, read expensive, for all parties involved. When the vendor is a listed company and dependent on transaction size, legal permissions may be required before the deal even gets to approval stage, never mind completion.

Largely, I can say with confidence that the longer a deal takes to progress, the greater the chances of failure. Also bear in mind the personal age and aspirations of vendors. The more mature vendor is likely to want a quick exit, cash in hand, while a younger vendor may be enticed with the promise of greater rewards in a new business opportunity.

ARE YOU A BUYER OR A SELLER?

What sort of a question is that to ask? you may be thinking. Surely, it's obvious: if you have something to sell you must be the vendor; if you are staring at a rather large gap in your portfolio, well, you must be the acquirer.

I hate to have to tell you that you could not be more wrong! Here's an example. You feel pretty sure you want to realise your investment. Perhaps your organisation has, in your view, reached its peak and the only way is down. Perhaps there is an economic dip in your industry and you aren't sure how you will weather this particular storm. Or perhaps you are just plain fed up and want a change.

This is looking distinctly like a sale, isn't it? But pause for a moment. You may want to sell your organisation now, but don't assume that it is necessarily saleable. Actually, everything is saleable so let's put it another way. You may not be able to sell at the right price.

One of several options presents itself:

- you could take a lower price (not ideal), although there are ways of improving on this;

- you could hang on and see if the market improves; or

▶

- You could become an acquirer (yes, I did say acquirer!).

One way of maximising the value of your organisation is to consider a 'buy-build' strategy. In other words, bolt on synergistic companies to make the most of what you've already got.

The rainmaker

Immortalised in the John Grisham book of the same name (*The Rainmaker*, 1995), this charismatic player in a transaction appears to be shrouded in mystery.

Certainly not an essential individual in the team, this character may become part of the mêlée by default. However, when they are retained, they can be quite helpful, since the rainmaker's job is largely in brokering the deal in the first place. An expert rainmaker creates a deal out of concepts or ideas, by knowing his market and understanding supply and demand issues. His ability to study the market and spot opportunities for introductions is an essential skill.

These skilled individuals will have identified a company's potential to be bought out by another business and will 'sell' the proposition to one or, if he is really shrewd, both parties. Like a marriage broker, he will be making the appropriate introductions to create a desirable union, one where the whole is greater than the sum of its parts.

If you are the acquirer or vendor you may be able to search out rainmakers but, more often than not, they will approach you. That isn't to say you shouldn't take a proactive approach but they rarely advertise their services and few rainmakers act solely in this brokering capacity. It may be that they are part of a general corporate-finance service so your professional adviser is probably the best place to start.

THE FEES

Rainmaking fees are also a fascinating area. It may not be all that unusual for the adept rainmaker to take a fee from both the acquirer and the vendor in the same transaction! Talk about conflict of interest! Yet that may not actually be a problem – at least for them!

To create a deal out of essentially what is only a conceptual idea takes huge amounts of time – not just months but sometimes years. The courting process alone could be lengthy.

And, even if a match may appear to be made in heaven, that doesn't mean it will be a successful union. As the instigator of the activity, the rainmaker in most cases takes fees once the transaction is completed, with the chance of an abort fee being scarce to nil.

Our rainmaker therefore has to ensure that those deals that do complete provide him with the windfall funding he needs to compensate for the far larger proportion of deals that will simply wither and die.

So, all things considered, don't expect these people to come cheap. Fees are usually a percentage proportion of the consideration, varying with the deal size. For very large deals this could be a fraction of 1 per cent, and for more modest deals 4 or even 5 per cent or more.

As you will discover as you read further, all deals hit hurdles. The able rainmaker will help steer a complex course, keeping all parties on track and maintaining pressure on other professionals to meet deadlines. They are often deal leaders and that alone can assist the chances of success as, at some point in a transaction, 'deal fatigue' is inevitable.

Corporate finaciers

In the absence of a rainmaker, these individuals are usually the deal leaders. Often but not always affiliated to an accounting practice of some sort, corporate financiers can be accountants, lawyers or industry experts, or may be qualified under the recent corporate-finance qualification run by the Institute of Chartered Accountants.

But the skills of the corporate financier are not judged merely on the letters after their names but on their contacts in the funding arena and their negotiation skills. Quality corporate financiers on both sides of the deal will make the transaction far smoother for both acquirer and vendor.

Unfortunately, lots of people dabble in corporate finance, participating in the occasional deal or fitting this around their day job. It's sometimes a sideline among tax advisers or auditors. Unless your deal is a modest one, these ill-prepared individuals are not the best choice for you. Part-timers do not specialise in leading the deal and, if the individual running yours has not got the experience of the highs and lows of transactions or seen first-hand the numerous reasons why deals fail, they are not best equipped to provide the rescue service that is often essential. Consider the following.

Corporate valuations are always a source of massive debate to both buyers and sellers. Furnishing the client with a sense of reality is very much at the core of the corporate financier's job. Clearly, those who carry out only a limited number of transactions have a more limited idea of market values. Although value, like beauty, is in the eye of the beholder, a full-time corporate financier will be able to provide a much greater insight simply by virtue of the sheer volume of work already accomplished in that arena.

Funding contacts can also make a substantial difference to your success rate. Although for the 'right deal' funding will nearly always be available, it may not be the best available if you haven't talked to the appropriate parties. Corporate financiers have to know the funders in the market and good ones will have not just local and regional but national and international contacts. They will know who is keen to fund particular types of deal and acceptable rates of interests as well as other, more obscure, facets of the art of deal making. They will also understand the whole process of acquiring the finance, know how to accelerate the process and be aware of what constitutes a nonstarter.

As many deals require a certain amount of debt leverage, some funders have specialist structured-finance departments. Corporate financiers become 'best friends' with the personnel in these sections. They are not the same as the general business banking staff and therefore only specialists tend to meet them. Their approach to risk may differ from the mainstream banking so they can, of course, mean the difference between deal and no deal.

However, perhaps the greatest skill a corporate financier has above others is negotiation skills. The ability to take a commercial view of a transaction is not something vendors and acquirers always have, possibly due to their emotional involvement. Lawyers rarely have it because of their need to provide absolute certainty of protection (naturally) for their client.

It is often therefore the job of the corporate financier to chair a debate into the pros and cons of a particular issue and to negotiate a way through deadlock to create a win–win situation. This may sound a bit of a cliché, but it is nonetheless effectively what occurs.

At times, transactions feel like nothing more than point-scoring opportunities among the parties. Good corporate financiers endeavouring to get the best deal for their clients can spend a considerable amount of time placating and reassuring all the parties in the deal. The process is traumatic for many people and corporate financiers often find they have turned into counsellors and emotional crutches for those who are sincerely struggling to keep their heads above water. I always spend as much time consoling and mollifying my clients during transactions, be they buyers or sellers, as I do structuring the whole deal.

I am told negotiation is a technique that can be taught, and certainly some critical principles can be absorbed and adhered to, but, on balance, I believe that a good negotiator is born, not made. Successful corporate financiers are always good negotiators.

Multitasking and time management are skills necessary for many professionals, but especially for the corporate financier. Deadlines are rarely met for completion, but that takes nothing away from the requirements of the corporate financier to manage the multiple and often conflicting needs of the main players in the deal.

These people need to ooze confidence and be able to reassure both clients and funders in relation to unexpected issues that arise. Your reliance on corporate financiers will be substantial at times. If you can't reach yours at a crisis moment, which inevitably will not be between 9 am and 5.30 pm on Mondays to Fridays, you have chosen the wrong adviser.

THE COST

Corporate finance fees are taken in various ways. For management buy-outs, nine times out of ten the fees will be wholly linked to the deal's success. In other words, if the transaction fails, our corporate financier gets nothing. (Shame!)

However, there is generally an upside to compensate for potential fee losses. Usually it is the right of the corporate financier to charge a premium on fees generated for a successful deal.

These premiums vary and they can be as little as 30 per cent or as much as 100 per cent. I recommend you have a maximum fee cap in your engagement terms. This will enable you to gauge more accurately the total maximum costs the deal may accrue.

Only on rare occasions are the fees not contingent. This may be due to a benevolent parent company underwriting the fees, or some of them, for the management buy-out team. This usually means the corporate financier has less room for manoeuvre on fee lifts as he has the security of at least a proportion of his costs.

Management buy-in advice is also usually done on the same basis, although sometimes high-net-worth individuals seeking

▶

to identify a transaction are prepared to pay for advice on an hourly basis. More often than not, however, a fee will be taken by the adviser on the successful completion of the deal typically linked to time costs with a premium in a similar way to the management buy-out costings.

For trade acquirers the process is usually different. Fees are usually quoted for each element of the process, for instance, identification and courting of target businesses; negotiation of the transaction, including valuation, finance, identification; and deal management. My advice is to get a clear breakdown of costs for each area. Ask for fee caps, though your adviser will usually insist on a 'chaos clause', which is a right to increase fee quotes if deal circumstances change dramatically.

However, even with this clause at least you will have a better idea of where your money is going to be spent. The scale of fees varies enormously, because, although deal size is clearly an issue, the skills of the advisers on the other side will also affect costs.

The best advice is to get a number of quotes from professionals in the corporate-finance world. Don't choose on price alone and remember that you have to work very closely with these people, so you must like and trust them. You need absolute confidence in their ability to do the deal, since you will be incurring costs anyway.

For fundraising activities the corporate financier may choose variable routes. It may simply be an hourly-rate-costed exercise, as in a trade acquisition process, or the whole or part of the fee may be contingent on a successful deal, often linked to a percentage of the funds raised. Again, percentages are often linked to the sum of money raised, with higher percentages for more modest sums, largely because the process is much the same if you are raising £150,000, £1,500,000 or more.

Disposals are generally costed in a different way. Dependent on client needs, there may be an upfront cost for the production of the information memorandum (IM) – a document that

▶

provides a detailed description of the organisation you are presenting for sale – and/or for a valuation plus the management of the whole deal. These sums vary dramatically according to advisers and size of deal, but expect to pay a minimum of £5,000 for a very small deal indeed, and much more for larger transactions.

The major part of the fee for the corporate financier for a disposal is taken on completion of the deal and is nearly always based on a percentage of the consideration, often levered to different rates if higher premiums on value are achieved. Again, no level of percentage strictly applies. It will be driven by deal value, but for an arrangement worth, say, £2,000,000, expect to hand over approximately 2.5 per cent to your corporate financier.

The two other activities that corporate financiers tend to get involved in are discrete or standalone exercises on company valuations and due diligence. Both these activities could be part of a bigger transaction or they could be simply distinctively independent activities. The cost of both tends to depend on what's required.

A valuation could be an extensive exercise providing multiple methods of deriving a possible business value based on investigation into deal activity in the sector. Alternatively, the valuation could be technically very simple and provide the user with only a basic insight. This is definitely 'horses for courses'. If, for example, you are the acquirer and you are just doing a 'look-see' at the general market, you may be wanting some outline valuation data on several deals just to gauge a feel of the possible opportunities. Equally, if you are seriously looking at a particular transaction or want an accurate picture of what your own venture is worth, you will probably want considerably more substance in the completed document. Choose the method to suit your need.

A general look-see at, say, a simple business turning over around £2,000,000 to £3,000,000 will cost about £3,000 to £5,000 maximum, but a comprehensive view of the same company backed by data research and so forth will cost double that. However, these are merely indicators, and you should always secure alternative quotes.

Be wary, though, because there are lots of cheap and cheerful options. I have heard of one organisation that promises to value a business for £250, a sum that usually equates to a professional hourly rate!

With regard to due diligence, corporate financiers tend to be involved in a multitude of ways. They may be appointed by the acquirer, to carry out a commercial analysis of a possible transaction, or by the vendor, to conduct a presale analysis. As before, ensure you have a comprehensive breakdown of the fee, who will do what and when you will receive the report.

Corporate financiers also work for funders to provide an independent review of the viability of a funding proposition. If you are the acquirer, this will not be your corporate-finance team (since clearly they would be regarded as having a vested interest in producing a favourable report) but will be a third-party firm that is funder approved. Your own corporate financiers will, however, work with you and the prospective funder both to scope the requirements and to negotiate the best fees for the work.

This work is never done on a contingent basis, as clearly this could create a biased view. However, it is not unusual to see a premium on time for a successful deal and an abort fee. Don't be surprised to know that either way these fees are for the attention of the acquiring company or team.

Corporate financiers involved in significantly larger transactions do, of course, carry out other functions related to floatations and public-to-private transactions, but for readers of this book activities such as these are probably for the future. When you get to that stage you need to take specialist advice from those corporate financiers who work specifically in that area.

Some corporate financiers specialise in industry sectors and, when your business is especially 'niche' (and these are truly only few and far between), use someone who has expertise in your commercial sector. By and large, though, the nature of the business is much less relevant than you probably think.

Finally, you should consider whether you'd prefer to use a discrete corporate-finance house, sometimes referred to as a boutique operator, or a corporate-finance department that is affiliated or attached in some way to your accountancy practice.

As always, there are pros and cons. The main advantage of using a boutique is that this is the sole area they operate in. That doesn't necessary mean they are better than a departmental corporate-finance team, but they have no distractions whatsoever. That said, the major disadvantage is that all other technical services often have to be bought in. The lack of these skills in house, however, doesn't mean there is a vacuum, merely they have to be accessed externally, and that may carry a cost premium.

Accountants, auditors and tax advisers

These people are usually integral to a transaction. Indeed they may be your first port of call if you are a 'virgin' to transactions or 'serial entrepreneur wannabe'. Even the most modest of business ventures requires the intervention of accountancy advice reasonably early in its life cycle. Therefore, most businesspeople are probably more comfortable with these professionals than any other. But there are three specific categories of accountancy staff who are quite different in what they bring to the deal.

Let's take the accountant first of all. Like transactions, they come in all shapes and sizes. They may be sole practitioners offering practical hands-on advice in relation to financial analysis. They may even be part of an investment team possibly taking up a nonexecutive position with the new company after the deal. They could, however, offer a more sophisticated impact to the transaction. For instance, if the accountant on your advisory team is linked to an auditing practice they could offer specific technical expertise on accountancy issues related to, for example, industry-specific queries. They may be able to assist you post-transaction, that is, with the installation of specified management information systems (MIS) required to ensure compliance with funders and subsequent conditions – in other words, requirements related to compliance matters linked to the funding provided.

Some accountants now provide assistance relating to human-resources (HR) issues. For instance they can identify jobs and people for the financial team and even help with the interviewing process.

This broad sweep of services and a widening range of providers mean costs will also be diverse. Ask for costed detailed proposals from at least two possible providers and check they have deal experience relative to the size of your transaction. Such fees are unlikely to be dependent on the deal's completion but, where they are, premiums will certainly apply. A lot of the work provided by the accountant is post-transaction and therefore it is generally your 'new company' that is paying their fees, though not always!

If you are looking for practical, real-time input, communication is essential. Sadly many accountants don't speak the same language as the entrepreneur and are often poor communicators. This means that, because you don't know what you don't know, you are possibly not asking the right questions and are not being properly informed.

When a corporate financier is on your team, he or she should be ensuring that such communication issues are eliminated; but, if you haven't one in your armoury, be wary of potential pitfalls. Share general issues with friends and colleagues who may have been involved in transactions themselves. There is nothing so useful as talking to someone who has been through the process on the same side of the table as you!

The role of the auditor is significantly different, largely being involved after completion. Not all companies need an auditor, and sole traders and most general partnerships don't need one at all. Only companies who meet specific criteria are legally bound to have their annual information audited – those with a turnover of more than £5.6 million, gross assets of more than £2.8m and more than 50 employees.

That doesn't mean you shouldn't have one; indeed, an auditor can help increase the value of your business.

In a nutshell, the auditor's job is to make a statement about the accuracy and fairness of a company's accounting information. Auditors work on behalf of the shareholders, not the company or the directors. In reality, the shareholder and the director may be one and the same person, but the roles are separated by law into two.

Like accountants, auditor outfits come in many guises: small and friendly, large and impersonal, proactive, reactive, specialist or all-rounder. The audit may be something you see merely as a legal compliance, or you may see the auditors as an integral part of the team. It is important to establish what you want from your auditors when you appoint them and to keep them up to date on any changes of heart.

Some auditors are more proactive than others, keeping you informed on technical and legal changes that may affect your business, encouraging regular meetings and organising training events. Others – in my experience the majority – often provide a passive service comprised of basic compliance followed swiftly by a bill for services rendered. If you have a first-class finance department and a strong, able finance director, this may be all you require. If you don't, avoid this latter type of adviser. Inexpensive, possibly, but the old adage 'you get what you pay for' is very relevant indeed.

Fees vary hugely for auditing services and, although you may like the idea of using one of the larger national practices, even if it's only to give credibility to your financial statements, you may find them outside your pocket for early-stage SME (small and medium-sized enterprise) ventures. Indeed, very often the big three or four players in this field won't really want your business and may cost themselves out of the occasion.

However, you may like to explore regional practices with more than one office. If you have high growth aspirations their expertise is potentially likely to be wider and deeper than small local outfits. Personal recommendation is valuable in identifying the right auditor both from a fee and a relevance perspective. Talk to fellow entrepreneurs and get a clear idea of charges – and don't be afraid to shop around. Even where you have made the appointment, this doesn't mean you are stuck with these auditors indefinitely. Carry out beauty parades every few years or so, particularly as your own business will benefit from a fresh approach.

Fees can be managed by improving your MIS and also by being clear on specifically what you want.

Specialist tax advisers can make the difference between an acceptable deal and a fabulous deal and this is so whether you are a vendor or an acquirer. Getting advice early in the transaction process is essential.

There could be massive tax implications linked to revenue clearance if safety nets aren't installed by a vendor prior to the transaction, and this is where the tax adviser comes into play. Consideration, no matter how well deserved, can be severely eroded by subsequent and unexpected tax demands.

From the purchaser's point of view, some transactions attract specific tax charges called stamp duty. This extra cost in a transaction can be managed if you are properly advised in advance of a valuation.

These advisers can also help with transaction issues linked to post-deal investments such as taking overseas residence, rolling over gains into other ventures and gifting of some proceeds, ensuring the tax paid is the absolute minimum.

Good advice doesn't come cheap and this is specialist advice, so therefore attracts premium rates. However, if the advice doesn't generate additional purchase or sale value, then you have chosen your advisers poorly.

Deal experience is essential, as are good contacts and relationships with local tax inspectors. Together these can speed up what can be an unwieldy process. And it's comforting to know your 'technical expert' is taking care of this complex and fast-changing area.

Costs are impossible to quantify – they are deal-specific as well as variable from a professional point of view – so getting comparative quotes is essential. Beware of selecting on price alone, however, since ultimately what you want is the best possible Revenue-approved tax structure, and that comes at a price!

Lawyers

Some people describe the lawyer as a necessary evil in a deal but this can be unfair, at least on occasions. In truth it's virtually impossible to complete a transaction without some legal intervention. The input the lawyer has in a deal can be variable. In a small deal it's tempting to use a lawyer in much the same way you would a corporate financier, to negotiate the deal for you. But here I have some words of caution. I have, on occasion, had to ask the lawyer to step out of the room at completion so last minute commercial decisions may be taken!

It is a rare lawyer indeed who will take the same commercial view of a transaction as the entrepreneur or corporate financier. Legal training alone helps to prevent this! This is not a criticism but it can become a problem if a lawyer negotiates the commercial terms of a transaction.

For instance, part of the lawyer's job is drawing up the sale-and-purchase agreement. A lawyer's job is to de-risk the vendor's exposure to potential claims.

The acquirers may want you to warrant or promise something about a historical or future event. Your lawyer will want you to make this promise only if you are absolutely certain of its truth. You may be subject to financial penalties, or worse, if the pledge you have given in good faith turns out to be wrong.

The fact is that, in many matters, there is never absolute certainty. That's when you will have to weigh up the risks you take by not giving this warranty.

You are probably thinking, Well, I am paying for this professional opinion, so why wouldn't I just do what they say? Of course you can but accept that it may mean losing the deal. Listen to legal advice, heed lawyers' warnings, but you, the entrepreneur, should be the one taking a calculated risk.

Just as there are branded accountancy practices that work on transactions, there are at least as many specialists in the legal profession. Substantial 'blue-chip' firms with fee structures to match are rarely going to be interested or even cost-effective in a modest deal worth up to £4–5 million.

However, do choose your lawyer with care. You wouldn't expect a painter and decorator to produce a Picasso. Well don't ask your matrimonial lawyer friend to work on a transaction. I kid you not – I have often seen things like this happen. If there's a nonspecialist on the adviser's team there can be untold problems.

Once you have the right one, you will see that your lawyer does have a proper place in the process of buying and selling businesses. The legal ramifications of getting it wrong can be horrendous! Above that, using an experienced commercial lawyer in the drafting of the numerous legal documents, which at a completion meeting can genuinely fill a room, not only gives a more secure deal but also a quicker one.

Experienced commercial lawyers ultimately know what is reasonable and realistic. Two good-quality lawyers (one on each side of the deal) may make a tough task of hammering out the details of the legal documentation, but it's also likely to be fair and speedy.

Accessibility to your legal team is also critical. No deals work to standard office hours. Email communication and the like is all well and good but nothing beats a face-to-face meeting across a table with your legal team.

Generally, legal jargon is scary and commercial legal-speak is no different. Often the entrepreneur is too embarrassed or simply overwhelmed to ask if his legal team would mind explaining just exactly what is an 'escrow account'. You will get an impression about whether your lawyer can communicate with you in a language you understand early on. If you don't know what the devil they are talking about and feel embarrassed to ask, get another lawyer!

Other people you know will have done deals, so look at their experiences and seek recommendations. Ask also about post-transaction relationships (always a telling scenario!).

Legal fees are invariably a point of interesting discussion. Whilst this must-have input rarely comes cheap, as with other professional costs, everything is negotiable. Some fees can be provided as part of a successful deal with a premium uplift (30–50 per cent is usual in management buy-out, or MBO, transactions). If possible, get a maximum-capped fee so you know your total exposure. Of course, the lawyer may just work on an hourly basis, particularly for corporate acquisitions, disposals and fundraising.

Be very careful in these circumstances, because fees on an hourly rate soon escalate. Remember, the hourly rate will be clocking up not just at meetings with you and your team but during telephone calls and backroom work. Without pre-agreement, bills can come as a horrendous shock. Get an idea of how fees break down prior to engagement.

Funders

A critical factor in many deals is the role of the funders – and I mean the funders themselves, not just their money! A big mistake I see with many would-be entrepreneurs is that they do not see their funder as a partner in their venture. In highly levered deals, the funder often has more money invested in the business venture than anyone else. It is essential, therefore, to treat him with care. However, this doesn't mean bowing down and pandering to his every whim. Instead find out right from the start what he wants from the relationship and make sure you provide it. If you can't, let him know in advance why you can't and when you will.

Poor communication is the kiss of death in a funding situation for both parties but usually a much more painful experience for the entrepreneur. There is a large variety of funders and they don't all have the same criteria attached to their funding provision, meaning they need to be approached and treated in different ways. The simple way of dividing funding groups is into two groups, those that provide debt and those that provide equity.

Debt funders come into the transaction with some security against their loan, for instance, a charge against your building or your debtors. That means if you default on your repayments they have the right to cash in on the named asset. On the other hand, they also want to continue charging interest on the loan. After all, that is their remit and how they make money. It is in the interest of debt funders, therefore, to keep lending to you provided you can continue to service that debt. In a worst-case scenario, they can, of course, sell off your assets to satisfy any outstanding amounts.

Debt funders now have a whole array of other products they encourage you to buy, from insurance to stationery, which illustrates that they are keen to build and maintain an ongoing relationship.

In cases where asset value is high and there's a history of good profit streams, the debt-banking market is highly competitive. Funders are as a body determined to manage the relationship in such a way that you remain with them as your funding provider.

Of course, if your business venture isn't that fortunate in terms of assets and profit streams, you will have only limited opportunities to negotiate on terms and conditions. In such cases it's essential to ensure you create a 'native' relationship with your bank manager: get them to be part of your team so they understand your business, its highs and its lows, and feel (you hope) more inclined to support you when business is not going quite so well.

GOING NATIVE

It goes without saying that you need to deal as much as possible with the 'movers and shakers' – the managers who, at best, make decisions that meet all your needs or who, at worst, can be highly influential with those who can.

For debt lending you may find you will be in either business

▶

banking or corporate, each division using distinct teams and dealing with different lending amounts, or who may even be industry specific. You may also find that, once a transaction is completed, these are not the same people who manage the account on an ongoing basis. So don't forget that, when you are doing the negotiations for your transaction, you must meet anyone else who will be involved post-completion. You must be able to communicate easily and get on with them all.

Finding out the credit-lending mandate of individuals is not easy (they themselves are often very reluctant to share this information) but your corporate financiers may have an idea. The rationale for this is simple: keep the decision about the amounts of lending to people you have a relationship with, and you have a greater chance of influencing the outcome. Where decisions have to be approved by third parties such as a credit committee, your chances of a successful transaction are no longer in your or your adviser's hands.

Your bank manager will have a number of clients to look after, often several hundred. It is important that they regard you as special, so you must work at the relationship, even when times are very good – in fact, especially when times are very good, because when they are bad you need the bank manager to remember the best of times and be supportive.

It may be pertinent to point out that when I ran my own company based in Yorkshire I banked in Lancaster. That is where the manager I had used for most of my own transactions transferred to – and I insisted on moving with him!

Institutional equity funders are a different species altogether. For one thing, they are very often not bankers, their whole view of lending being quite different from that of debt funders. An equity investor is less interested in security and ongoing interest and more in the short- to medium-term opportunity to make a substantial return on the capital sums invested. For this purpose most institutional equity investors take three to five years as an ideal investment term with a minimum expected return on their investment of 35 to 40 per cent per year. Of course, that isn't to say they will eliminate risk entirely from their selection criteria but it is not part of their primary decision-making criteria.

However the funding from these organisations is introduced (see Chapter 8) it will almost always be the right of such organisations to have a seat on your board in the form of a nominee nonexecutive director. His job is to represent the interests of the funders. You may or may not have the right to nominate this person but you should ensure you have some input into the selection process. Sometimes this may be an employee of the institutional lender but it is more likely to be an independent whose reputation the investor respects.

When things are not going well with an investment, the nonexecutive director is often seen as a go-between, liaising between the board and the investor. An accomplished professional will be a mediator acting in the best interests of the company, but sadly not all are high-calibre. Still, it is obvious that this person will be a fairly critical component of the business infrastructure in the future should matters not go according to plan.

Equity investors feel very like spouses at times. Sometimes you will love them to bits and at other times you won't be able to stand the sight of them. The trouble is it's very difficult indeed to get divorced in either the good or the bad times. If everything is going well they will want a large premium to exit and if fortunes are dipping no one will want to bail them out. So the moral is, choose your bedfellow with care!

Independent financial advisers

Useful in a disposal to provide investment advice for the sums you realise on exit, independent financial advisers, or IFAs, often provide many other products and services, including keyman cover, shareholder-protection insurance, life cover and pension and mortgage advice.

There are thousands of such people or organisations, so lack of choice is certainly not an issue. The industry is heavily regulated and disclosure of commission and fees now mandatory, so you will have a very clear picture of costs versus benefits before making a commitment.

As with other professionals, I suggest you get quotes from at least a couple of providers before making a commitment and thoroughly read the presentation. Make it acidly clear what you want and ask for all candidates to present recommendations against the same critical outcomes. That way you will be comparing like with like.

This market has had its fair share of bad publicity and some providers should be avoided. Careful preparation means you won't make a wrong choice. As usual, personal recommendation is a good place to start. Your corporate financiers, lawyer or accountants, or even your funder, may have endorsements to make. The ongoing relationship with the IFA is usually not quite as critical as with other professionals, but you do need to feel comfortable with their professional ability so don't accept the first option. Remember, always link their wisdom to relevant tax advice, as some products will be tax advantageous and some won't. So these professionals need to work together to advise you on the best scenario.

Try www.unbiased.co.uk, which gives details of IFAs and what they can do.

Your family

Although your family come last in this list of parties in a transaction, there is a strong argument to make that they are actually the most important. There are various theories about separating your work and your personal life, but this is one area where a division is going to be tricky to orchestrate.

Instinctively, I feel that your family will be involved directly or indirectly. Bringing about a transaction, be it a sale or a purchase, will be a traumatic process and I would challenge anyone to keep their business-related highs and lows apart from their family life.

If that is at least accepted in principle it makes sense to make family members aware of the whole scenario and, better still, to let them help you through the painful process.

Apart from being a happy distraction, just having someone to listen to your issues can enhance your ability to cope. Sometimes, your nearest and dearest are linked into the prospective deal whether they like it or not.

It is entirely possibly that the family's own financial security may be at risk. If you are a buyer, for instance, it might have been necessary to sign a personal guarantee, which by implication could affect the retention of joint assets. So it is better to bring them aboard.

As deals are often protracted, there will be times when transaction issues impact on family occasions such as holidays and weekends, since there is rarely enough time for those involved to manage issues within conventional business hours. Although you may be in the habit of working long hours, imagine doubling your workload and dealing with it in the same time span. Advance warning to the family – and reminding them that this is a transitional process – will, I promise, help you and them.

Of course it doesn't all end once the deal is completed – in fact sometimes it's just the start – but the pressure post-transaction is different entirely. Either you have the worry of running your own company or you are left wondering what to do with the time and money left on your hands after selling a business.

So keep your family close, air and share concerns and take time out of the deal-making process to spend with them.

PART 2

Buying

Chain of events for a typical purchase

This is not a strict order and some events will naturally run concurrently.

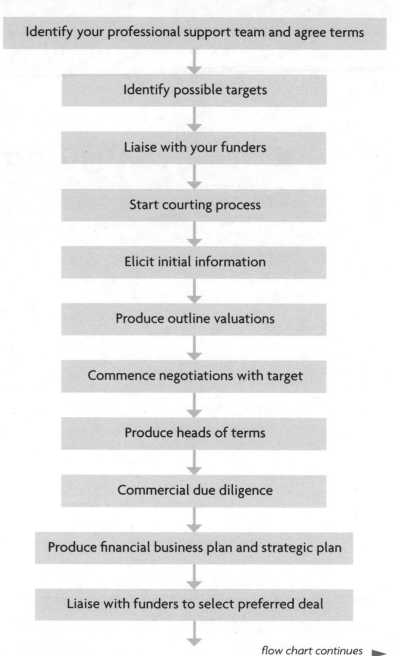

Identify your professional support team and agree terms

Identify possible targets

Liaise with your funders

Start courting process

Elicit initial information

Produce outline valuations

Commence negotiations with target

Produce heads of terms

Commercial due diligence

Produce financial business plan and strategic plan

Liaise with funders to select preferred deal

flow chart continues ▶

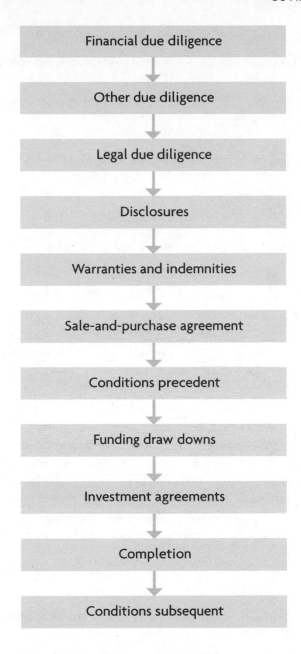

NB: the process is very similar for an MBO/BIMBO, except target is already identified.

CHAPTER **3**

Finding the Right Business to Buy

THERE ARE ANY NUMBER of sources for the would-be acquirer to access, from dedicated websites to regular publications. However, what these don't show are those businesses not being actively marketed, but which would be for sale should someone make an approach with the right offer.

In my experience in the SME sector, virtually every business is potentially for sale. The problem is that the owners may not know it and, of course, nor may you. Often, the best businesses for sale are those not actually on the open market. Indeed, often those that are on the Web, in the newspaper or business-for-sale publications are there only because all other routes to find a purchaser have been exhausted. Practically, therefore, your logistical routes to find a suitable company to buy are as follows.

- Scan the relevant websites and businesses-for-sale magazines and make initial contact with the vendor or broker to confirm an interest, requesting relevant information.

- Let your professional adviser know you are inclined to make an acquisition. Your bank, lawyer and accountant will all potentially have contacts and knowledge of the market.

THE BRIEF

Provide the broker with a clear scope – I cannot tell you how much this will help. Think about the following criteria:

- where the new business needs to be located;
- its size including turnover;
- staff numbers;
- industry sector;
- any particulars such as loss-making (yes you may feel you can do a turnaround);
- growth market;
- high-tech/low-tech;
- lack of management team or first-class management team;
- sound asset base;
- what sort of funds your business may have at its disposal.

But, if you really want to be proactive, you need to appoint a corporate financier or rainmaker to make approaches to potential suitable companies on your behalf. Using specialist databases and having an insight into mergers and acquisitions, they will know whom to approach and how to approach and, more importantly, understand the chances of turning an initial enquiry into something more exciting.

Once again, it is absolutely essential that you brief these people thoroughly. Often they will be acting for you on a contingent basis, which means charges kick in only when the real discussions start. But, if you have instructed full-blown research, you may be being charged accordingly. In order to make the most of this service, your instructions must be clear.

A huge number of acquirers ask me to identify, a company –

any company! With such a vague brief it is impossible to know where to start. The problem could be that you don't know exactly what you want because you don't know what's available. Take a big step back and carefully explore your motives and goals before you embark on the whole process.

These are inevitably going to differ, since, as they say, you can't know where you are going until you know where you are.

If you are a personal acquirer or management candidate ...

You know already from this book that if you fall into this category and don't have serious personal wealth or very modest expectations, you have the hardest of all routes to a successful deal. But if you are committed, and this is something you really desire, then here are some of the things you may want to consider in addition to those covered elsewhere.

The first is that there's **strength in numbers**. Would you have a better chance of success if you joined up with others, in other words, increased the size of your team? This would give you both greater buying power (more funds) and more time, since there would be a number of people to share the load.

Set yourself a **time limit** to secure the deal. Be generous and double your estimate of just how long you think is reasonable in the first place. I have known people spend three years or more looking for a deal!

Get yourself known in the financial community – network madly and gain creditability by demonstrating your abilities and knowledge.

Use the time wisely while you are looking for a transaction. Expand your skills by learning another language or improving your IT skills.

Write your personal **five-year plan**.

If you are a corporate acquirer ...

Create your 'must-have' and 'desirable' **target company profile**. Consider carefully what it is you are **seeking to achieve**. Fundamentally this may be more products into your market or a greater market arena for your products. Of course, you could be seeking to diversify, which, trust me, will present a huge new challenge.

Once you have got a clear idea of your desired outcome assess the **financial capability** of your own business and begin outline discussions with your funders, initially your incumbent banker (later on you will talk to third-party funders).

Get your **management on board** for the transaction and make quite sure your goals are as aligned as possible with your top team.

Write a **clear action plan** with your senior management that fully explores the pros and cons of an acquisition and deals with the perceived risks and challenges. This will impress your funders and will help you all prepare for the journey. With the failure rate very high for both carrying out the transaction in the first place and post-completion failures, it's important to remember that failing to plan is planning to fail.

CHAPTER **4**

What Are You Buying?

T HE TITLE OF THIS CHAPTER is a question that will perplex entrepreneurs, and is definitely one that should be posed before completion. The one I sometimes hear after the deal is done is, 'What have I bought?' and it is far less fun to answer.

As well as the tax issues related to what you may buy, you need to understand what each possible option means and also how this may affect value. Entrepreneurs buy organisations for different reasons, related not only to a desire to succeed personally, but to secure a competitors' brand, access other markets more successfully than a startup or to steal market share from a rival.

For this reason, it is important to think carefully about the different options.

Assets

An asset is essentially something owned or is owed. Examples include buildings, plant and equipment or fixtures and fittings, these being known as fixed tangible assets. In addition a business may have intangible fixed assets for sale, such as brands, intellectual property (IP) and goodwill.

The other type of asset typically for sale would be what is

called a current asset. This could be debts (that is, money due from customers for products and services rendered), stock or work in progress, and even cash reserves. In accounting terms, a current asset is one that should be realised within 12 months

Often when carrying out an asset purchase the acquirer is also, curiously, buying liabilities owed to third parties such as creditors, bank loans and overdrafts, and outstanding Revenue and Customs payments. When a transaction is carried out in this manner it is called a net asset deal, in other words the assets residing in the business and all the liabilities create a net amount of the sums due.

In addition to the value of the asset in relation to market value and realisation prospects, you should also consider its replacement value, especially if this is a deteriorating asset such as plant and equipment, stock or fixtures and fittings.

ASSETS HAVE DIFFERENT VALUES TO DIFFERENT PEOPLE

I sold a business once with virtually no 'book value' but a huge amount of specialist equipment, which essentially allowed the owners to produce unique products. These had substantial value to the acquirers. They were specially made many years before and virtually irreplaceable. However, to an unrelated buyer they may have had only break-up value.

Shares

When you buy shares, you buy history. Effectively, it's a transfer of ownership and what that means is any residual issues within the company are automatically switched across, as essentially the ownership of the company has just changed hands.

These issues can be positive and negative. The positives include such things as tax losses and rebates, while the negatives include product and service liabilities and Revenue and Customs errors, all of which will be your responsibility.

Vendors always want to sell shares, since by and large this is much more tax-effective, while acquirers usually prefer to buy assets. Due to this dilemma, there is always lots of negotiation and, for a variety of reasons, you may have no choice but to purchase shares. With this in mind, you need to be aware of the issues related to such a version of the transaction.

When you buy shares you are to some extent assuming a responsibility that you may be unable to copper-bottom through due diligence. However, with potential risk like this in mind, buyers can try to seek extensive warranties and indemnities from the vendor. The vendor, of course – equally wishing to limit his own risk – will be seeking to minimise such promises.

A share deal can be for the total quantity of issued shares or a fraction of these. That fraction is of vital importance not only in relation to value but also in terms of control over the business activities. For instance, a 51 per cent stake will allow the holder to pass only ordinary resolutions whereas a 75 per cent stake will allow the holder to pass a special resolution, a significant weapon in her armoury.

It is entirely possible of course, to have all sorts of different classes of shares within a business. The most usual are ordinary shares. These simply represent a proportional share in the company and attract a pro rata right to vote and a benefit from any dividends. But this simple type of share can be amended to reflect different types of ownership rights, including preferential voting and dividend rights and even buyback rights (the right to have the company purchase back the share at a given time and even a given value).

So astute buyers need to ensure their purchases are managed to take into account the ramifications of the different shares in issue, including the owner's right actually to sell the shares to anyone other than a specified party.

Staff

Regardless of whether you buy shares or assets, you have, as acquirer, little choice in the fact that all those personnel employed by the business you are purchasing have to transfer to your control. This requirement is covered under the TUPE regulations we met in Chapter 1. This Act – the Transfer of Undertaking Protection of Employment Right Act – allows employees to enjoy exactly the same terms and conditions as they had with the previous employer under new management.

The transfer has to be what is called relevant. To determine this, two questions need to be answered:

1. Is there a stable economic entity that is capable of being transferred?

2. Will that entity retain its identity after the transfer happens?

TUPE will therefore tend to apply in the following circumstances:

- sales and mergers of businesses or business assets;

- changing contractors;

- changing of licences or franchises.

It will not apply in only very limited circumstances, including

- where assets are sold but the business itself is not a going concern;

- where the transfer is situated outside the UK;

- where any employee has less that one year's service.

The other really important change in the law is that, from April 2005, pension rights also transferred. That factor might add greatly to the cost of transactions.

There may appear to be a raft of negative issues here, but there are, of course, lots of potential positives.

Very often the real value of an acquisition rests in the skill of the personnel who work in the organisation. Their knowledge and personal relationships are often beyond measure but can make the difference between a successful deal and a disastrous one.

If this is the case, it is vital to hook critical personnel into the future of the business. This could be via a sound service agreement, although these have only limited value – when someone genuinely wants to leave a job, she is demotivated and no longer an asset. However, at least you may have some breathing space to try to effect a handover.

A SENSE OF BELONGING

Provide employees with a sense of ownership. Allow them to participate in the deal (see the discussion of BIMBO deals in Chapter 2) or set up a specific share-ownership scheme such as an Enterprise Management Incentive (EMI) scheme or Phantom share scheme, both of which give workers a different perspective on the future of the business as they become part-owners.

The EMI Scheme, which was introduced by the Finance Act 2000, is a more tax-advantageous route for the employee, as it allows the people who are eligible to own shares and therefore take advantage of the tax relief available on sale. However, these schemes may have to be approved by Revenue and Customs and there are certain restrictions on value and trades that qualify. Seek specialist advice before embarking on this route.

A Phantom Share Scheme, on the other hand, tends to be more flexible, as no actual shares are given but rather a bonus is paid out, determined by the increase in the value of shares.

This can be Revenue-approved or not and can be set up informally, so making administration and establishment costs fairly minimal. It is important, however, to provide a transparent mechanism governing share valuation. For further information on these schemes see my previous book, *The Business Rules*.

Know-how

Know-how is probably the trickiest element of a transaction to evaluate, yet – like those people who are an intrinsic part of a deal – the expertise within a business may be essential for its future. Know-how is a technical expression of knowledge and can include manual and intellectual skills. It is the knowledge or skill required to carry out a function or provide a service.

The problem? This knowledge often rests with the very people who are selling the business and therefore may not remain with the company for the medium or even short term. Of course, if essential know-how is in the head of the vendor, business value is going to be adversely affected. For you as a buyer, the transfer of that knowledge either to yourself or others remaining with the organisation you purchase, is pivotal to future success.

KEEP A PAPER TRAIL

One client I recall had what on paper looked like a fabulous company, although small (turnover £1 million) it made over £750,000 a year net profit!

Unfortunately, the owner had no written resources to support his costings, designs or customer contacts. In fact, he didn't even have a fax machine, let alone a computer! Needless to say, the value of this particular business did not reflect its outstanding profit record.

The due-diligence exercise of you as a buyer should ensure you are comfortable that critical information in terms of running the company is at least transferable and that you have a method of ensuring that this transfer actually happens.

Where know-how is held in people's heads, this may not be easy to orchestrate, but you need to consider these issues in relation to appropriate handover and training procedures.

Customers and contracts

Sometimes an acquirer may seek to buy a particular business merely to get access to its customer base. Perhaps it includes customers who would be interested in products he can access that the existing business doesn't currently offer. His best route to presenting these products may be via this acquisition route. This is particularly so with many blue-chip companies, whose buyers are notoriously difficult to access.

It could be that by gaining access to these customers you then neutralise opposition by simply removing the product currently on offer and replacing it with your own.

Sometimes customers will contract with a company for a given period, albeit with certain covenants attached to that arrangement. This contract could, provided terms are adhered to, provide the acquirer with a guaranteed income stream (always a comfort after completion!).

However, carefully check these contractual covenants, particularly for such clauses as 'change of ownership' and general novation rights (that is, the right to transfer ownership of an asset, lease or contract to a new party).

A clause of this nature essentially means it is at the behest of the customer whether or not they continue to purchase products or services from the new owners. In addition, in an asset purchase, these contracts almost certainly will not automatically transfer.

PUTTING ALL YOUR EGGS IN ONE BASKET

Be careful also in relation to customer dependence. In most cases the Pareto economic principle applies: 80 per cent of the company's business will rest with 20 per cent of its customer base. That doesn't mean, however, that you would or should feel comfortable with any business that has more than 25 per cent

▶

of its income being dependent on one customer, however blue-chip that customer may be.

One client of mine had a successful company with 95 per cent of its business linked to one organisation. It was a high-street name that he had worked with for many years, although no contracts were in place to guarantee this would continue. Despite its exemplary profit record, this meant his company was virtually unsaleable.

As a buyer, also be wary of customer relationships based on the provision of unsustainable discount structures, unrealistic rebate schemes or those based on personal relationships with exiting vendors.

Suppliers and contractors

The purchasing of a supplier relationship or contract is not dissimilar to that involving a customer. You may think that it is entirely possible to negotiate terms of supply with anyone; unfortunately that simply isn't the case.

Some suppliers will, for instance, have solus relationships with particular customers, in other words, a dedicated relationship with just one organisation, due to geographical or size restrictions or even distribution agreements, and, therefore, access to a particular product may be possible only by acquisition of the whole company. Once again, watch out for change-of-ownership clauses in such agreements and unrealistic terms and conditions.

If the supplier is providing you with a manufacturing service, be vigilant about who owns any intellectual-property rights and watch out for penalties related to cancellation rights.

Brands, intellectual property and goodwill

When a premium on net assets is paid for a company (see Chapter 6) this often relates to the acquisition of that intangible asset, which is often referred to as goodwill. The value placed on this is, in part, hugely subjective but may be more easily quantified if it can be linked to a specific brand, a protected trademark, a design or a copyright.

The valuation, of course, is still subject to interpretation but the fact that it has been afforded a degree of protection in, for instance, the registration of a patent should make the buyer feel more confident in its longevity and sustainability.

Intellectual property (IP) is found in four main areas:

- patents – for inventions, for instance;

- trademarks – to allow for brand differentiation;

- designs – for the appearance of a product;

- copyright – for such things as literary and artistic materials.

From the acquirer's point of view, registration of these in a legal format is critical, as is the geographical coverage of the registration. Nonpatented products may be legitimately plagiarised and the value of the concept eroded or even completely devalued.

Also, as an acquirer, you should be aware that simply registering a patent does not give you an absolute right to sell a product. A patent stops others copying your products but the sale of your patented item could infringe someone else's rights.

These are very specialist areas and, where a transaction value is based on intangible assets, you need to take appropriate advice on the validity of the item and also on any potential ongoing plagiarism or litigation related to it.

Also, you could as the new business owner find yourself liable for offences under the various laws related to 'copycat' antics, including the very serious common-law offence of 'passing off' – marketing your product as a 'unique brand' while, in effect, it looks suspiciously like another.

You should also be aware of the taxation issues related to goodwill, which were amended in the 2002 Finance Act. These changes allow companies to obtain tax relief on the purchase of intangible assets provided they were purchased before 1 April 2002. The company who own the IP will also be able to select the rate at which they write off this goodwill for tax purposes. However, there is a maximum period allowable for non-brand IP, which is 25 years. If you purchase a brand and this can clearly be justified, as it must be every year by your auditors, it may be possible to leave such value on your new balance sheet indefinitely.

FRANCHISES

One of the safest ways of owning a business is through a franchise. Defined as the provision of a licence or similar legal authority to provide a service or goods within a particular geographical area, a franchise comes with the ready-made trademark, operating system and marketing package. The failure rate is, compared with that of a new startup, very low. More than 90 per cent of all franchises are still in business 12 months after purchase.

It is possible to purchase a franchise in virtually any business sector, from training and development and a variety of sevice sectors to almost any type of retail product you could possibly imagine. There are thousands of options to choose from and one of the best places to start is the British Franchise Association (BFA). This national body, whose job it is to promote ethical franchising, is a membership organisation that provides advice and structure to both franchisees and franchisers. Although not all franchise operators are members, most quality organisations are likely to be.

Not only does franchising offer you a substantial choice in business type, but the costs of buying into the system in the first

▶

place are variable, from a few thousand to tens of thousands of pounds.

If you select a model recognised by the BFA, you have a degree of certainty about the quality of support you will be given, which should include initial and ongoing training and marketing services as well as a wide range of other management support such as bookkeeping and product development.

Most franchise fees are twofold: initial costs for the purchase of the franchise itself followed by ongoing fees, often linked to either turnover or gross profit. All terms are laid out in the franchising agreement, which will be unique to that organisation and will contain commitment requirements from both the franchisee and the franchiser.

The size of the market in the UK (over £10 billion) and the statistical information on the high success rates make this an appealing investment not only to operators but to funders. The five main high street banks all sponsor the BFA website.

If you have a buy-build strategy for your business, franchising your own organisation is a possibility once you have established your offer and procedures. The BFA run regular courses not only for franchisees but also for would-be franchisers and provide ongoing advice and assistance on recruiting franchisees and maintaining and developing your network.

Entrepreneurship is probably mostly about risk taking. Franchising offers the would-be entrepreneur the opportunity to take a rather more calculated risk. It allows the owner-manager to run a company but have the benefit of a much bigger support network both in the riskier startup phase and in the future.

CHAPTER **5**

Getting the Vital Information

WHEN YOU BUY A BUSINESS you are buying potential, and
therefore you have to apply a degree of subjectivity in
defining what that may be worth. But the more information you
have about your prospective purchase, the more confident
you will be that you're paying the right price for the right
company.

CONFIDENTIALITY

Corporate financiers are generally paranoid about keeping business transactions concealed until the client gives the go-ahead
for deal data to enter the public arena. Sometimes I feel as if
I work for the secret service!

Just like military top brass, corporate financiers frequently
give each assignment a code name, for instance, Project Scorpio
or Project Lincoln or Project anything, in fact. The aim is to
ensure that only those directly involved are in the know.

The rationale behind such furtive behaviour is fairly obvious.
For buyers or sellers, leaked information about a transaction can
change a deal – although I use the word change intentionally,
since it could be positive or adverse, depending, of course, on
which side you are on.

▶

Every business of any size will have confidential information, be it a list of customers or secret formulae for products. Often, a substantial proportion of business value will be enshrined in the documents containing this information.

So a vendor is more than a little concerned to ensure these do not pass into inappropriate hands and that – if they do – the vendor will have a legal course of action to remedy it.

It is usual therefore, that vendors always require the purchaser to sign a nondisclosure agreement (NDA). This agreement creates a legally binding contract, prohibiting the buyer from poaching staff, for example, or plagiarising products. There may be other restrictions on professional advisers who perhaps need access to the data for, say, valuation purposes.

Just because there is an NDA, however, it doesn't automatically mean it will be enforced. A breach might occur because the information in question is not confidential in the first place. Then there are action costs to consider. Sometimes devastating damage is done by a leak but the task of bringing litigation is onerous.

That said, it would be a foolish vendor indeed who allowed a would-be purchaser access to critical business information with nothing in place to prevent its misuse.

For a buyer – particularly in an auction-type deal – an NDA should also provide a greater sense of security post-transaction (if they are the successful party), as the losers in the race haven't had uncontrolled access to critical business intelligence.

Although you do not need a lawyer to draw up an NDA, it is a legal agreement and so drafting needs care to ensure it is correct and enforceable.

As a potential buyer signing an NDA, check if the agreement is mutual or one-way. Check also the exact nature of what is regarded as confidential and of any time frames on disclosures. Above all, keep a copy for your own records and advise everyone working with you on the transaction of your agreement, because, by implication, they may well be linked to it.

Although there is a whole raft of information you must review, there are some very specific documents that need your utmost attention. Don't rely 100 per cent on lawyers to do the job for you. They may pitch in too late so that you incur unnecessary costs.

Articles of association

The articles of association govern the activities of the business – for instance, how directors are appointed and what quorum is needed for legitimate decision making by the board. The latter is of particular importance, as it is the directors who will make recommendations on whether the shareholders should consider a sale or not and, naturally, to do this, they need to have a board meeting.

You should read these thoroughly – and I suggest you do this when you are wide awake and alert, as they can be chock-full of jargon. If you do spot areas that appear inappropriate, for whatever reason, amendments can be carried out prior to an acquisition. But shareholders need to pass a special resolution to allow this to occur and that requires a 75 per cent vote in accordance with the particular articles.

It goes without saying that you must check whether any particular shares have different voting rights from those of other issued shares.

Every company must be registered at Companies House and a copy of its articles of association is kept there, making the information available to everyone.

Shareholders' agreement

The shareholders' agreement (see sample in Appendix 8) is an entirely different animal from the articles of association. It is not available in the public domain and, unlike the articles, which bind all shareholders in the company, a shareholders' agreement ties up only those shareholders who sign the agreement.

Like the articles, shareholders' agreements are full of legalities and tend to be lengthy, so a quick review is rarely an option. However, one fairly critical point is the right of pre-emption. Pre-emption rights effectively allow all or some incumbent shareholders, or indeed the company itself, to purchase any shares offered for sale at terms stated in the agreement before the third-party acquirer can assume control. A vital point to consider is that your possible acquisition might be scuppered because a single shareholder exercises such a right.

Drag-along clauses and tag-along clauses also need special care, because, if a shareholder owns more than 10 per cent of the shares, it is possible they may not necessarily have to sell their shares. A drag-along clause can change this in varying percentages, dependent on what was agreed. The tag-along clause gives the shareholder the opportunity to sell her shares when others are being sold at not only the same time, but the same value.

There may also be share option schemes and phantom option schemes in place, often subject to a different agreement from those of other shares, but nonetheless these may have implications for the new owner, as the rights attached to these shares will almost certainly rest with the individual concerned. Under the TUPE regulations, these rights and obligations could certainly transfer to the new owner.

As basically anything could have been written into a shareholders' agreement (provided it was legally contracted and is not illegal in itself), each one is unique. In more complex businesses, it is possible that there will be several classes of shareholder, each with different rights making negotiation with the vendor challenging to say the least.

I had a client, a 70 per cent shareholder, who was convinced he would be able to persuade his other shareholder (who owned 30 per cent of the shares) to do what he wanted. Big mistake – particularly since she was his wife! No amount of persuasion or generous offers from the acquirer would persuade her to sell.

Statutory books and records

All companies have to maintain a set of statutory books, these include:

- the register of past and present directors and company secretaries;
- the register of shareholders and of their shareholding;
- a register of debenture holders and other mortgages and charges (that is, charges held by third parties against company assets);
- a register of any directors' interests in shares or debentures of the company;
- minutes of board meetings;
- shareholders' minutes.

All shareholders have the right to look at shareholders' minutes and the public in general have the right of access (for a fee) to the shareholder register.

The company must also retain certain other legal documents including its

- certificate of incorporation;
- copies of the articles of association;
- directors' services contracts.

All these should be kept at the company's registered office – which may not be the same as the trading office. Indeed, in smaller organisations, the registered office is often the business's accountants' or lawyers' premises. In any case, it must always be a named place. It cannot, for instance, be a post office box, since it is a legal requirement not only to keep these documents but to maintain them. Any changes, for instance, in directors or shareholders or charges given must all be kept up to date. As a buyer, therefore, you will be able to track any important movements in both personnel and securities.

If these records have not been maintained properly, there is a breach of company legislation. Although on the face of it you may think this a minor misdemeanour, I have been involved in many frantic processes at completion as statutory books are hastily written up, often delaying the completion. Worse still is when share certificates are absent, because the transaction is delayed for unacceptable periods.

For one completion meeting I recall, the vendor, who was based in the USA, got on a plane with the share certificate in his briefcase and travelled across two time zones to reach the meeting – not on time. In other words, no share certificate, no completion.

Health-and-safety records and policies

A surprising number of director disqualifications are related to health-and-safety breaches. In addition to substantial fines that can be levied against companies who break this extremely far-reaching legislation, there is also the possibility of incarceration for the perpetrator and the managers and directors above him.

Even assuming some protection via warranties and indemnities from the vendor, a would-be acquirer should at the very least be satisfied that comprehensive policies and procedures are in place and that breaches are being recorded and policed in the appropriate manner.

Health-and-safety legislation applies to all premises not just factories and laboratories. Indeed, in office premises the dangers may not even be obvious: think trailing computer cables or storage of hazardous substances such as printer toner; even poor lighting and ventilation are health-and-safety issues.

As policies apply not just to those staff that work for the company but visitors and even the local community (for instance, in relation to emissions), this is clearly not just an internal issue.

For offices and shops you need to ensure that registration with the local environmental-health department has taken place, and for factories that registration has taken place with the Health and Safety Executive.

As a minimum you need to see:

- the health-and-safety policy;

- appropriate risk assessments;

- employee welfare procedures.

And of course you also need to be satisfied with the employer's liability insurance cover (the only circumstances where this isn't needed is if all the employees are close relatives).

You must also be sure that the vendors have communicated these policies to their employees and that adequate training is provided for all staff. Indeed employees generally have a legal right to be consulted about health-and-safety issues that affect them.

For companies employing more than 20 people you will also need to ensure there is a fire certificate, particularly if the company you plan to acquire provides direct access to the public, such as a restaurant.

I also recommend you look at the accident book. RIDDOR (the Reporting of Injuries, Disease and Dangerous Occurrence Regulations) require that particular injuries and diseases are reported.

The accident book ideally should record all accidents, however minor.

Employee records

Getting access to the details of these before due diligence, and sometimes even before completion, is unlikely. Unsurprisingly, vendors are always concerned that an unscrupulous would-be acquirer may simply be on a fishing trip to access their valuable personnel. However, since there is so much value in a business in the quality of the people who work for it, understanding who and what you are getting is fairly crucial.

Bearing in mind this is advice for the acquirer, not necessarily for the vendor, here are the details you should review *as soon as possible*.

A company organisation chart showing numbers of personnel in each section. This could give you, the acquirer, a quick feel for where possible savings could be made – especially so if you have a company already in which you wish to absorb your new acquisition.

Contracts of employment. The standard used by the company with notes on any unique contracts that are in circulation.

Director service contracts and nonexecutive contracts for service. Where these exist they are likely to be more comprehensive than the above employment contracts.

Critical points to look for on all contracts are:

- notice periods from both parties;

- guaranteed bonus payments;

- guaranteed salary increases;

- working hours;

- pension rights;

- sick-pay rights in excess of statutory rights.

I had one client who didn't check these in full, only to find he had to give five years' notice to one member of staff, whereas the employee in question had to give only one month.

Also look at:

- job descriptions;

- appraisal information (in particular look at training records and target achievements);

- what is expected from the staff and what has previously been agreed;

- disciplinary information.

To access all this latter data you may need permission from the employees concerned. There is obviously value in seeking this information sooner rather than later, if you possibly can.

CHAPTER **6**

Valuation Techniques

I F YOU HAVE TURNED TO this chapter first in the hope you will instantly discover the knack of how to value a business accurately, then you will be sorely disappointed! Valuing a private company is more akin to a black art than a black-and-white science.

This chapter will provide an insight into some of the techniques professional valuers have in their toolkit. But at the end of the day a private company is worth what the vendor will sell for and what the acquirer will pay (subject to his having access to the funds, of course).

Some methods are more complex and others more applicable to particular businesses. No single method is correct and, once you have gone through the whole process, it is almost certain that the actual price you pay will be different from the one initially touted, due either to the negotiation process or to the various factors likely to be revealed in the due-diligence process.

The other problem with valuing a business is that I can almost guarantee that the vendor will have unrealistic expectations about what his business is actually worth. In simple terms, vendors value high, acquirers value low.

There are also some issues relevant to a valuation that are pertinent only to a particular buyer and a particular seller. Synergies that are available to one acquirer may not be available to another, so that acquirer may be in a position to offer a greater value than another. A typical example might be that you, the acquirer, believe that, when you purchase this particular organisation, your current infrastructure will wholly support it, allowing you to make drastic savings on overheads and people. In simple terms, you can make two and two equal five, and, in order to gain access to this business, you are willing to pay a premium on value that another, less synergistic, buyer cannot achieve.

But be wary and very cautious in reviewing your potential 'savings', since my experience is that these rarely or sometimes never come to fruition and there's always a delay or unforeseen cost in the integration process.

In terms of coming to an initial valuation, which will almost certainly change throughout the process (both up and down), you need a whole raft of information (see Appendix 2) to come to the first tentative figure. Almost certainly, this will be based on fairly broad assumptions, which will need to be validated at a later stage (as much as you are able). This might include estimates on customer retention, contract renewal and the general value of assets such as stock and work in progress, debtors and buildings. For this reason the professional valuer may consider a varying array of valuation techniques and those described later are a sample of the more commonly used methods. It is worth considering the various methods for your own purposes.

Often the offer you make will be made across a number of scenarios. For instance, it may include some immediate payment to the vendor while further sums are possibly payable later, subject to verifying conditions.

In summary, valuing a business is only part of the process in a deal; actually completing the transaction – even finding a funder – is a totally different matter. I have even known vendors take considerably less than the seemingly largest offer for what seems fairly arbitrary reasons – such as the culture of the acquirer or, even more randomly, a personal affinity with the new management team.

SOME SPECIFICS

Valuations are often made on the basis of past performance, but in reality a purchaser is interested in the future. The fact is that previous results are of real value only if they provide a reliable indication of what lies ahead, so a business that has a volatile history can make a technical valuation more difficult.

Various factors affect a company's value, but, on a technical basis only, the four basic factors are the earnings (profits), dividends, asset value and cash generation.

Other issues that need consideration include:

- the general state of the economy and the industry in question;

- whether you have a willing seller;

- the abilities of the management team;

- issues such as dependence on customers and suppliers and indeed the quality of those resources.

In addition to utilising the internal information specified in Appendix 2 to carry out your valuation, you may choose to review this alongside published data. This could include:

- the FTSE share indices;

- trade directories and magazines;

- special reports that may be available on the industry (Jordan's Business Surveys in London, for instance, provide surveys on specific industries and sectors);

- online databases (some of which only your advisers may have access to, such as Corp Fin and Zephyr, which track international deal action; but some of which non-advisers may access, including Lexis, which contains legal information, Experian, which contains company data, and Jordan's, which provides detailed information on the financial status of 2 million registered companies).

As you start to firm up on the valuation via the due diligence process you will want to look further at:

- Corporation Tax returns;
- P35s (the record of benefits paid to employees);
- stock valuations;
- aged debtors and creditors;
- customer and supplier listings;
- insurance records;
- professional valuation of property etc.;
- contingent-liability information;
- brochures, catalogues and website information.

You may also want to meet the auditors, lawyer and even bankers, but all this is likely to be made available only to serious suitors who are engaged in progressive discussions and have entered into heads of terms at least.

Price–earnings ratios

Price–earnings (or PE) ratios express the value in terms of a multiple of profits. So one way of estimating the value of a business is to consider how much profit it makes and apply a multiple to these earnings. Two critical questions should come to mind: what multiple? and which profits?

What multiple?

The average multiple on profits achieved for businesses sold in the private sector as opposed to the public sector would logically be different and lower, after all public companies by and large are much more substantial but the gap in PEs has in fact been closing over the past two years.

The publicly quoted data can be tracked via the *Financial Times* reports, and BDO Stoy Hayward produce an interesting index on a quarterly basis available on their website, called the ·Private Company Price Index (PCPI), which tracks the average PE on all recorded private company sales. At Q3 2006, the FTSE all-share is at 13.2 and the PCPI is at 13.4. This compares with a much broader gap in 1999, when the FTSE all-share was at 29.1 and the PCPI at 13.

This could indicate an appetite for private company transactions but you should bear in mind that the PCPI figures include data for a wide-ranging collection of companies, some of which will distort the real underlying potential multiple you may have to actually pay.

A 'quick and dirty' guide to finding an acceptable multiple for you to apply could be as follows.

1. Identify in the *FT* listings a company similar to the one you are seeking to value. For instance, if you are wanting to buy a chain of convenience stores you might select Morrison's PLC. Now clearly your target is not going to be identical, certainly not in size, but remember that this is a short-order valuation.

2. To reflect this size difference, once you have identified the PE (listed next to the name of the company every day except Monday in the *FT*), apply a discount of 40 per cent to this figure and you have your first 'stab' at finding a profit multiple. If there are several businesses similar to yours listed, you could take an average of these.

The professional adviser is likely to 'firm up' this fairly speculative multiple by verifying real-life deal values on their database, such as Zephyr.

Which profits?

The PCPI and the FTSE all-shares are based on profits made after tax and these are where you should start. The next question is, are we just referring to this year's profits or last year's, or even next year's? Once again, in order to provide you with a quick method of carrying out this exercise I would suggest the following process:

	Current Year 07	Previous Year 06	3rd Year 05
Profit after tax	500	400	300
	×3	×2	×1
	1,500	800	300

Total: £2,600/6 = £433

In other words, this provides you with a weighted maintainable profit after tax, that is, a skewing of the profits towards the most current year. It would therefore be this figure to which the multiple you have identified would be applied and your first basic valuation achieved.

There is an immediately recognisable possible flaw with using these profits when valuing an owner-managed company. Profits in these businesses tend to be rather more fluid than in others. Expenses might be incurred that would be avoided if the business were in the hands of another owner (I'm thinking here of owner-directors being paid extraordinary salaries, for instance). You may therefore wish to review your definition of profits taking such issues into account.

A further definition of profits utilised by valuers is called normalised EBITDA, standing for normalised (that is, removing extraordinary costs – or even adding) earnings before interest, tax, depreciation and amortisation, which is the writing down of intangible assets.

Once you have established these figures, the purpose is to consider that the interest, tax and depreciation process you use will not necessarily be the same as the vendors', but that a similar weighting exercise can take place.

It is almost certain that the average weighted profits will now be somewhat higher and therefore the multiple applied should usually be lower. As a matter of course I would apply a discount of about 60 per cent instead of the 40 per cent. Alternatively a good rule of thumb is to use a multiple of between 3 and 6. Remember that these valuations (normalised EBITDA) are usually done on what is called a debt-free, cash-free basis. By this I mean that the offer you will make to the vendor will assume that any excess cash in the business will be added to the value and that any debt (such as loans and overdrafts, but not trade creditors) will be deducted from the value.

Net assets and goodwill

The last examples clearly take no account of the value of any tangible assets, such as building, stock and debtors, that reside in the company. If after you have completed the price–earnings multiple the newly derived value turns out to be less than the sum of your total assets, less your total liabilities, there's an obvious difficulty. Rather than do the deal, the vendor could simply sell off all his assets, pay off his liabilities and be left with more than the multiple.

Valuing a business in this way means a review of the actual value of the contents of the balance sheet is necessary. Technically, assets such as buildings, land, plant, equipment, fixtures and fittings are valued at cost price less depreciation, giving you what is called net book value (NBV). But, nearly always, NBV does not equate to market value.

Assets in accounts statements are generally under- or overvalued. Land and buildings don't generally depreciate, while plant and equipment, fixtures and fittings rarely have the same realisable value as hoped for (would you buy a second-hand desk?). With regard to these assets, known as fixed assets, the valuer needs to consider the depreciation policy used and, for the purpose of the valuation mechanism, restate their estimated market value.

Most balance sheets also contain current assets. These include stock and work in progress, debtors (the money owed to the firm by its customers) cash, etc. As with fixed assets, the actual value of these may not be the same as the book value. Debts may not be collected, stock may become unsaleable and, once again, a review of true value must be undertaken. Since a net-asset purchase usually assumes that liabilities both long and short will be deducted from the above assets, the same philosophy with regard to value applies. Are all the stated creditors payable, for instance? Are all liabilities properly accounted for, such as tax and customs duty? Once this review of both assets and liabilities has taken place and a more market-acceptable net-asset figure arrived at, then a starting point for this valuation has been reached.

The clear omission in all this is the potential value of the goodwill within the business being sold. Goodwill exists in all manner of areas, including brands, IP, trademarks and know-how, but how do you value it?

Of course the answer lies in what is acceptable to both parties in the deal, but it's a tough call. As one client told me, measuring goodwill is 'like valuing the potential for fairies at the bottom of the garden'. We may like to think they exist but where is the proof!

From a purely technical point of view, though, a simple way to determine goodwill value is to multiply the weighted-average last three years' profit after tax by three. The summary of this final valuation is therefore as follows. Arrive at a market-acceptable net-asset value to which you add your goodwill value using the formula above.

Discounted cash flow and payback

Cash generation is one of the most important elements in a quality business. Another oft-used alternative to evaluating the worth of a venture is to consider how quickly you will recoup your funds from the cash the new venture creates.

This is called payback. An acceptable payback period depends on the commercial view of the entrepreneur and his funders, but three to five years is usually the maximum. That said, in one deal I recently completed, the acquirers accepted a 14-year payback! Extraordinary, but they had reasons of their own, not least that this was the only company for sale in their sector and they wanted it very badly.

To enable you to carry out a realistic payback valuation, you need to have cash-flow forecasts that are as accurate as possible. The words accurate and forecast seem like a contradiction, but remember: I am talking of cash-flow forecasts, not profit forecasts – entirely different animals.

The trouble with all this of course is that the value of the pound in three or five years' time will not be what it is today. Its value then is anyone's guess, but I can guarantee it will be worth less than it is today, not more. To account for this, therefore, a discount factor is applied to the free cash determined in your forecasts to evaluate what the time value of the cash may be. An example is as follows, taking three years as an example.

| | 2008 | 2009 | 2010 |
	£000	£000	£000
Free cash flow	1,000	1,200	1,400
Discount factor 6.5%	0.94	0.88	0.83
Value of future cash flows	940	1,056	1,162
NPV (net present value)	3,158		

This means that the true value of the cash is not £3,600,000 but £3,158,000.

For the example I have chosen 6.5 per cent as the discount factor. The valuer would have to consider a percentage figure dependent on the economic circumstances at the time.

Special techniques for certain types of company

All sorts of factor will eventually affect the valuation. Here are four of them.

- Why is the owner selling and the buyer acquiring?

- What is the quality of the product's market, and market share?

- Has the company got some difficult or impossible to replicate technology?

- Can you, as the new owner, increase value exponentially?

All these factors, along with specific valuation problems – such as 50/50 or minority shareholders, property and farming companies, asset-rich and loss-making companies – will all skew standard valuation techniques. It is because each company has its nuances that ultimately, except for very small transactions, some specialist guidance is required. This is especially so if valuations need Revenue and Customs approval for things such as employee share schemes.

But what you have in this chapter are some very simple guidelines to start you on the road to evaluating worth.

THE ACTUAL VALUE

The actual value is of course the ultimate 'deal done' value and it could be for the vendor less than desirable (but, then the vendor doesn't have to sell!), and for the acquirer more than he wished (and, likewise, he doesn't have to buy).

NEGOTIATING THE TRANSACTION

This is not a book about negotiation techniques – appropriate manuals are available in abundance – but, as you will have ascertained from the valuation discussion, the ultimate price you pay for your acquisition will be a negotiated one.

Ideally, the negotiations will bring about a satisfactory conclusion and often this requires a great deal of creativity on the parts of the parties or their advisers.

My top tips on negotiating a transaction from the acquirer's point of view are as follows.

- To establish credibility as quickly as possible, unrealistic opening gambits such as derisory offers should always be avoided.

- Have a walk-away figure in mind. Deal fever is as abundant as deal fatigue and you may find yourself carried away with enthusiasm or sheer desperation to do the deal, making concessions you are later likely to regret.

- Have 'must-have' and 'wish' lists of things you want to achieve.

- While you still want to do a deal and it remains within your means, keep talking. Walking out of discussions after the proverbial teddy has been thrown from the cot won't help your credibility and never improves your chances of doing a deal. This is not the same as giving in. It's about logical and realistic discussions.

- Do not let a lawyer negotiate the value of your deal or the funding of it. By and large, their view will not be commercially the same as yours.

- Do not humiliate or talk down to the vendor however inept you may think she is. She can't be that bad if you want to buy her business. Business is personal for most people, whatever management books say, particularly owner-managed business.

- Seek to win the major objectives and concede minor ones; this helps the vendor have a sense of some goals scored.

- Let your professional advisers play the 'nasty cop' to your 'good cop'; this gives you room for manoeuvre in case you need it at a later stage.

- All deals are mercurial and not even binding until all relevant documents are signed. Renegotiation on critical issues with the vendor for no good reason, sometimes called brinkmanship, may look clever and may win you a cheaper deal, but people who play these games, particularly the professionals, get a poor reputation. You may not care too much if it gets you what you want. But one of the best ways of accelerating a fair deal is to put yourself in the shoes of the other party. One sure-fire way of upsetting, destabilising or collapsing a deal is to embark on a point-scoring exercise. It's not pleasant and generally it's not necessary.

- That said, no great entrepreneur plays with all his cards on show. Hold back some concessions until you feel you need them, and give in gracefully.

- Negotiate on neutral territory, since this gives both parties a degree of comfort and avoids unnecessary interruptions.

- Keep reconfirming positive matters that are agreed, since this gives vendors a sense of movement in the transaction and allows clarification of possible misunderstandings by both parties.

Checklist: information required for valuations

- Statutory accounts for the last three years for the companies being disposed.

- Management accounts to date (or relevant trading information).

- Current-year budget versus actual (if available).

- Future projections.

- Details of major customers, contracts and orders.

- Details of any property and the most recent valuation if the property is being sold as part of the deal. Is the book value significantly different from its market value?

- Details of plant and machinery, age, original cost and current valuation.

- Are any assets held under finance or operating leases?

- Articles of association.

- List of shareholders.

- Any shareholders' agreements.

- Details of any share transactions within the past six years and number of shares sold/transferred. Price of shares at date of transaction.

- Details of any legal actions/disputes that have been settled in the last three years or are outstanding at present.

- Details of directors' remuneration and other benefits for those leaving the business.

- Any other contingencies that you feel would impact upon the value.

- Details of any nonrecurring costs going forward.

- Details of any intercompany trading and management charges.

CHAPTER 7

Structuring the Deal

I F THE VALUE OF A DEAL is negotiable, the structure of how the consideration is paid is hugely variable. The job of the acquirer's team is forging the structure of the transaction so it is acceptable to both parties and also to minimise the risks to the purchaser so they don't end up buying something that later turns out not to be quite the business they had anticipated.

Many risks are managed within the legal framework, but some financial exposure can be reduced if you structure the way the consideration is paid to the vendors. Some vendors want cash and an immediate exit. Some acquirers seek a non-cash offer with all sums being paid to the vendor based on the subsequent business performance. In most private company sales, neither of these scenarios is acceptable, so a halfway house is usually the answer.

Astute acquirers recognise that vendors will be amenable to a deal that provides them with the most secure funds possible in the shortest time. On the other hand, most vendors wish to maximise value, so an incentive-based deal that allows them to reap the benefit from an increase in the value of the business post-sale may be of interest.

Deals can take many different shapes. However, here are some of the more usual structures, each with its own pros and cons for both sides in the transaction.

Total consideration payable in cash at completion

If the sums are right, this leaves you with a very happy vendor. They have no concerns you can't or won't pay, and no security issues. Their biggest problem now is what to do with the money. Provided the vendor has owned the shares for two years or more, they should, subject to revenue approval, pay a capital gain of only 10 per cent.

The pros for the acquirer are that this is a 'done deal', so there are no concerns about security issues regarding any unpaid sums, nor does the vendor have rights over how you run your business.

Of course, the big drawback for the acquirer is that all the cash must be found straightaway!

All paper (shares)

Sometimes vendors are given the opportunity to take the sale proceeds wholly or partly in shares in the acquiring company. When the acquirer is a listed blue-chip company, this may seem desirable for the vendor, especially if no restrictions are placed on the subsequent sale of the shares and they can be sold when the market is right.

But there probably will be timeframe restrictions on share disposals and, as we all know, shares can go up or down and might even plummet before the vendor has a chance to sell.

Of course, it could be that the acquirer is not a listed company but a private business. Taking shares in someone else's private business is highly risky in terms of discerning the correct value and cashing in on it. In addition, the vendor is likely to be a minority shareholder so is unlikely to have any influence in running the company.

Mixed cash and paper at completion

Sometimes this is a desirable option for the vendor, particularly if there's a desire to retain a sense of ownership in the new venture. From the acquirer's point of view, this structure reduces the gearing on the deal. The same disadvantages exist for the vendor, however, which is realising the value in the paper as and when required.

All-deferred consideration

From the vendor's point of view the only time I would recommend this sort of deal is if there is no other option available. However, deferred consideration can come in variable format.

Vendors' loans

For more detail of these, see the next chapter.

As the acquiring party, you may have found the company of your dreams, even agreed a fair price for it. The problem is that you cannot pay the vendor immediately because you can't persuade a funder to lend you all the money needed. Deal off? Not necessarily. More and more deals are done on the basis that, after a total price is agreed, the vendor doesn't take all his funds out of the business immediately but becomes a creditor to the business he has sold, redeeming the loan over an agreed period.

The vendor will certainly want to negotiate security of some ilk. The best on offer will be a bank guarantee. This means the vendor is assured payment should the acquirer default on the payment schedule. Unfortunately, the bank will almost certainly take this into account and deduct it from any security it may hold, so it is going to work only if you have excess security available.

As an alternative, it is possible, though a very limited option, to secure insurance against deferred sums. One provider of this policy is Deferred Finance Limited (DFL), 13 Austin Friars, London EC2N 2JX. These people will not necessarily agree to guarantee the consideration. It is an analysed choice on their part, and it certainly isn't cheap. However, it could make a deal happen that otherwise wouldn't. I have known some vendors pay the premium – and it is possible to finance it with another company to spread the costs, which often have to be paid upfront for two years or more.

A third option could be a loan to the vendor that, should default on the payment plan occur, enables him to take back some or all the shares he sold. It provides a shield for his exposure to risk. This convertible loan instrument will be complicated to draw up. And there are numerous issues attached to it, not least that a vendor may not want the shares back from a business that can't make its loan repayments.

Very often vendors concede on all the above on the basis that these issues are either unavailable or too expensive and complicated. The alternative is to take a risk in relation to the loan redemption. However, the vendor will certainly ask for interest-on-loan discussions – usually I start negotiation at about 1 to 3 per cent above base from the vendor's point of view and 1 per cent below base from the acquirer's, usually ending up somewhere about base rate.

In terms of redemption periods, these can be anything, but rarely go beyond five years. When advising the vendors, I would want to secure interest payments on a regular basis, usually quarterly but possibly half-yearly or even annually.

Vendors very often request the right to have a seat on the board up and until their loan is redeemed or at least have right of veto on certain items such as capital expenditure until the loan is repaid.

Deferred-contingent consideration

Now this is a much more risky position for the vendor, since he must put his money where his mouth is. The concept behind this structuring means that the acquirer pays the vendor further sums when criteria are agreed. These benchmarks can be virtually anything, including profit or sales targets, client retention, contractual success or even staff retention. The critical issue for both parties is the ability to quantify correctly whether or not the said agreement has been achieved.

My advice to everyone is to avoid basing deferred-contingent consideration on net profit. Even with extensive discussions to nail the formula, there may still be disagreement about when a pay-out is due or whether targets have been met.

From a vendor's point of view, a sales target is easier to quantify. But, from the acquirer's point of view, clearly anyone can sell £10 for £5, so you may be less satisfied with this. Whatever agreement you end up with needs to be crystal clear for everyone's sake.

When a deal is done on this basis, the vendor almost certainly will want some sort of proactive role in the company to allow scope for his personal management. He will also need guidance on tax implications to ensure such payments are treated as capital and not income.

Time spans are of course negotiable, but experience says these should be as short as possible, to preserve the sanity of both vendor and acquirer. Horror stories abound about old ways meeting new ways in a very disagreeable manner.

Partial share buy-backs

Unless both parties want a joint venture or plan to release some equity to an institutional investor, a partial acquisition by an acquirer is going to be fraught with problems.

It needs complicated shareholders' agreements, which will require discussions on valuation of shares that may be redeemed at a later stage, as well as death-in-service issues. These, along with complicated voting rights attached to minority shareholding, make it a less attractive option for an acquirer – unless of course it is the only option!

Consultancy agreements and employment contracts

Often it is essential to retain the vendor on a practical basis within the company post-completion, either as an employee or on a self-employed basis, to effect the smoothest handover. In either case, advice about tax is vital, and consideration also needs to be given to the accruing of general employment rights.

Usually, I would recommend that these agreements be for minimal periods from both parties' points of view. Whatever the terms are, though, ensure both parties are absolutely clear on what is expected and what rights are given. This pre-discussion and documentation will help later on when the inevitable disagreements come about.

The legal framework

You will no doubt have realised that lawyers play an important role in the transaction market. Generally, they enter the process midway through the deal rather than during commercial negotiations. Involving lawyers in the deal structure insures against potential legal implications that may arise.

My recommendation is to let your corporate finance adviser structure the deal in principle, then run it past the lawyers for them to scrutinise for compliance and revision. The legal framework of any transaction can look complex to a virgin deal maker, which is why it is essential you use a lawyer experienced in transactions that are similar in size to your own.

The plethora of legal documentation is mesmerising, in terms of complexity of language and the volume of paper. Here is a summary of some of the documentation you will encounter and tips on what to look for. It may not all be generated by the lawyers, but it all has legal implications.

The order of documentation as detailed below is quite usual.

1. Nondisclosure agreement (NDA) or confidentiality agreement

Although these appear fairly standard agreements, they are legally binding documents and therefore a signature creates a contract between the vendor and acquirer that, if broken, could spark a legal action. It will also bind others within your team who haven't necessarily signed it but are bound by implication to its terms.

Don't forget that these terms extend for lengthy periods: months, sometimes years and even indefinitely. So you need to ensure you keep this record somewhere safe, and that you manage the process to ensure compliance. Although actions brought about by breaches are rare, I would advise you to be very cautious, because penalties can be weighty.

2. Letter of intent and heads-of-terms agreement

These documents, which are in effect the initial offers and conditions made by an acquirer, can and should be relatively brief. They are not as important as the sale-and-purchase agreement. Bear in mind, however, that some elements of these initial documents outlining the offer are legally binding – for instance, the period of exclusivity offered to the acquirer to pursue the transaction along with various confidentiality agreements.

Unqualified personnel, sometimes those directly involved with the transaction or, alternatively, corporate finance advisers, often draw up these agreements. Either way, ensure you understand the implications.

Although brevity is the name of the game, salient points, known as the 'spirit of the deal', need to be described in these documents, and changes in the key terms are not well regarded by professional advisers.

Critical points include:

- cash consideration;

- payment dates;

- details of any deferred payments, for instance, when, what, how, security;

- critical due-diligence specification such as access to information, confirmation of contracts;

- personal terms for vendors, such as service agreements.

These heads of terms are usually then used to create the structure of the sale-and-purchase agreement. If the deal is complex and deferred sums are being utilised, it is worthwhile letting your lawyers and tax advisers have sight of these to advise on any negative implications.

3. The sale-and-purchase agreement

Probably one of the most complex legal documents in a transaction and certainly one of the most important, this should always be drawn up by your legal team (that is to say the acquirer's legal team). It is usual for this to be the most detailed legal paperwork with 'black-lined' (that is, amended and further-amended) copies going backwards and forwards between the lawyers while seemingly inconsequential legal issues are hammered out.

However, as this is the critical document that in effect transfers the shares or the assets to you, the acquirer, it is clearly important that you be entirely happy with its structure and the commitments that are being made by all parties.

Each sale-and-purchase agreement is of course unique to a business, but the critical factors are that the vendor owns the shares or assets and has the right to sell them and that the acquirer has the right to acquire them. Within the agreement there are all sorts of other sections, which include the detailed structure of how the consideration will be paid and any security offered.

It will also contain confirmations of issues such as authority to sell shares and statements on matters such as taxation, assignment rights, costs and confidentiality, along with agreed announcements and notices. It will also establish the governing law and jurisdiction.

A TIP

One particular clause that you might find the vendors wish to enclose is an anti-embarrassment clause. Vendors often suffer an awful sinking feeling that they may be selling out too soon for too little reward. One method of managing this issue, at least from the vendor's point of view, is with an anti-embarrassment clause. It allows a vendor to participate in any sale proceeds should the new owners sell the company within a given time scale.

For instance, if you sell a business you have bought, making a large gain on your original purchase price within a short period, the original owners can take a share of that increase. This is usually a staggered amount over a defined period so an exiting vendor couldn't expect to be awarded the same percentage 36 months after the original completion as he would in, say the first 12 months.

It isn't possible to give you specific percentages, as this is a negotiable element of each transaction. However, if this is a contract clause, acquirers need to be vigilant because to sell on within the specified period would mean having to share any gain with the original owners.

And watch the wording very carefully, because the sale date may not actually be completion, and the period could actually commence on, say, agreeing heads of terms.

But, if the sale-and-purchase agreement itself is important, the schedules attached to it are crucial. These of course will also be variable but as a standard will include:

- the seller's warranties;
- asset documents;
- data-room documents (if relevant);
- working-capital statements;
- completion documents.

4. Seller's warranties

From the vendor's point of view these are examined in more detail elsewhere in the book, but for the acquirer these are essentially statements of fact made by the vendor that make key assertions, such as, 'We own this brand.' Without these statements an acquirer is governed by the law of caveat emptor (or 'buyer beware'). In other words, you get what you buy whether it's good or bad.

For this reason, 'future warranties' that provide against things occurring in the future are given only reluctantly by the vendor, as control over forthcoming events is spurious. A typical warranty you may want to secure is that all book debts will be realised in 90 days.

Against any warranties that have been agreed, the vendor will make certain disclosures. So one warranty may be that there is no outstanding litigation against the company, save for a disclosure that outlines a particular scenario which is attached. That disclosure means that the acquirer will have no right of action against the vendor linked to the scenario as its existence has been disclosed (if the acquirer has agreed to accept that disclosure).

Where risk is seen by an acquirer as likely, she may request the vendor provide an indemnity. The essence of this indemnity is the provision of funds laid aside by the vendor in a specific account (called an escrow account), which the lawyers on both sides of the transaction manage and from which payments are made if the indemnity is called upon. From the acquirer's point of view, the crucial difference between a warranty and an indemnity is that the warranty will require pursuing a case though the courts and all the risk that entails. With an indemnity, the funds are already set aside.

These issues require substantial legal input, as vendors want to provide the minimum and acquirers want the world! A compromise is always needed and a commercial standpoint is essential.

5. Asset documents

There may be original or certified copies of items such as hire-purchase agreements or purchase invoices providing details of assets on the company's balance sheet and, at the very least, an asset register. It may also contain stock records and debtor listings.

6. Data-room document

Where the sale process has been managed via an auction process, all those documents made available in a data room may form part of an agreement, particularly where warranties have been made.

7. Net-asset adjuster

Sometimes transactions require a statement that gives the vendor an additional sum of money post-completion, called a net-asset adjuster. It means that, once the sale has been finalised, completion accounts will be drawn up and any difference in the assets of the business between one date and another will be paid over to the vendor. Conversely, if the figures have reduced, the vendor must make a payment to the acquirer. These criteria could be linked to an agreed computation on what working capital levels are acceptable in the business.

This will require input from corporate financiers and accountants. From a vendor's point of view always get a pound-for-pound adjustment up or down on these net assets and agree that the accounts will be drawn up prior to completion of the transaction.

AND DON'T FORGET THESE!

One critical document that acquirers will definitely need (even those who think they don't) is a shareholders' agreement (we

▶

discussed these earlier), essential unless you plan to own 100 per cent of the shares in your venture.

These agreements – which are often overlooked – control the changes in ownership of a corporation and are binding on the parties that sign.

Shareholders' agreements should always be written in the early stages of the transaction, since this is when you and fellow shareholders are likely to be most friendly and so more receptive to negotiation.

They usually control the following decisions:

- whether a departing shareholder must be bought out and on what terms (that is to say, who and at what price);

- what if anything would trigger a buy-out, for instance, the death of a shareholder, or her retirement or resignation from directorship.

You may also want to consider what would happen if the shareholder divorced or was declared bankrupt.

Here are some tips on the creation of these.

- Make it clear who is the potential acquirer if a nominated event occurs. Is it the company or the other shareholders, or either or both?

- Always have a valuation mechanism in the agreements. In all the years I have been involved in this area the biggest disputes relate to share value.

- Consider the need for 'good' and 'bad' leaver clauses.

- Always get your lawyer involved in writing these documents but negotiate the commercial terms yourself with the help of your corporate financier.

- Don't forget that such documents bind only those shareholders who sign them, so it is essential if you plan to have further shareholders at any time that you have a deed of

▶

adherement. This essentially forces new shareholders who may come into the equation to abide by these terms.

As an acquirer of the business, you will probably, in addition to being a shareholder, also be a director and an employee.

As an employee you are entitled to an employment contract within eight weeks of commencing work for the new business. But as a director you are well advised to have a director's service contract. This includes all areas covered in a standard employment contract but also recognises certain peculiarities about the position of a director. These include the right to access all important commercial information.

Other key clauses your lawyer should advise you on include:

- the job title and purpose;

- salary and bonus details;

- expenses allowable;

- holiday entitlement;

- sickness and disability rights;

- pension matters;

- restrictive covenants;

- confidentiality clauses;

- IP rights;

- hours.

Your lawyer will advise you on the reality of critical clauses such as restrictive covenants. But, if yours is a levered deal using funding from an institution, the content of service agreements will by and large be in the hands of the funder, who will be vigilant about benefits and salaries not being excessive until they have recouped their investment.

8. Money-laundering documentation

As a result of the money-laundering regulations that came into force in 2003 you will find it virtually impossible to engage the service of a professional adviser such as a lawyer without completing the procedures that the FSA require all professionals to institute prior to engagement.

So expect to produce your original or a certified copy of your passport or driving licence, plus at least one further official document such as a utility bill, showing evidence of your name and address. In addition, if you are acting corporately your adviser will search Companies House to pull off your statutory records.

The point of this procedure is so your adviser is confident of the identity of his client. If any funds used in the transaction turn out to be unlawful, he will reveal the relevant details to the authorities.

9. Investment agreements and facility agreements

Where your deal includes third-party finance, in the form of either equity or loans, agreements about them must be drawn up and signed. These will contain a barrage of conditions, a breach of which could cause a default and allow the funder legitimately to seize his cash.

It is possible that you'll have several such agreements from the various funders involved in your deal. So be sure to set up a monitoring process that will help in compliance or will at least flag up potential breaches in good time, either to stem the violation or to enter negotiations with the funders prior to their taking reversal action.

Other than the conditions subsequent and precedent and various other covenants, investment agreements often include the right to appoint nominee directors to represent the funder at board meetings. Ensure you have input in the selection process, as you will be paying for this privilege.

10. Completion documents

These are likely to be multiple and variable but may include things such as board and shareholder resolutions (agreements), board minutes, articles-of-association amendments along with company and director registration documents. All rather technical and definitely destined for the lawyer.

CHAPTER 8

Finding the Finance

YOU MAY NOT NEED cash to buy a business, indeed you may not need any cash at all (well, at least not your own). Generally, you will need some sort of finance – but finance doesn't necessarily mean cash.

Typical sources of finance

External third-party funding comes in two specific ways: via loans and via equity. But within these two models are a hundred and one variations. One of the most important factors in securing funding is to ensure you match the need to the product – in other words, borrow the right kind of money, not just the first type offered to you, because this may come back to haunt you.

Short-term debt

1. Overdrafts

Overdrafts are the most common facility, available widely from any high street bank. This is a flexible product and meant for funding short-term working capital. It is a simple agreement between you and the bank that allows you to borrow up to an agreed amount. In return, you agree to pay interest and a service fee. Expect also to pay for the setting up of the facility.

Provided you use an overdraft correctly, this is cheap financing, as interest is calculated on a daily basis, so you pay only for what you borrow. Overdrafts are ideal for seasonal businesses or companies with an account that moves in and out of credit on a regular basis. Quick to arrange, they can often be secured over the phone. The necessary security documents are fairly minimal: a debenture on the business assets may be sufficient, but occasionally a personal guarantee will be required.

However, an overdraft is usually what's called an on-demand facility. Although it's unusual, it means the lender can withdraw the facility at any time with no notice. As you usually have to renegotiate every 6–12 months, there is no certainty of renewals and, of course, there is a fee every time the facility is reintroduced.

Interest rates are variable, dependent on the risk perceived by the funder. It is unlikely you would be granted less than 1 to 1.5 per cent over base rate for a young business, but that is where you should aspire to be in an ideal world. Reality says it will be 2 per cent plus. I have known a company pay 7 per cent over base. This was a restaurant – a very high risk, at least in the bank's opinion – but even for a new business, anything over 3 per cent over base is high.

In terms of set-up fees, this is a negotiable area. Often it will be a flat fee or sometimes a percentage of the facility. The best way to gauge value for money is to get competitive quotes and use them as a lever.

2. Credit cards

Yes, I have known plenty of small businesses fund their company by borrowing on their personal credit card. Just about anyone can get a credit card with no proof of earnings necessarily required and with no security needed. The trouble is that the crushing interest rates often reach the percentage teens, but, if you pay them off before the payment date, it is effectively free credit.

It may be that the credit card you use is a business rather

than a personal one. These come with a company credit category and have access to greater reporting services (that is, information of the use to which they have been put) and even complimentary insurance and discounts.

3. Credit lines from suppliers

One of the most frequent sources of business funding is that of late payment to suppliers. This seems to be something of a national pastime and – within reason – it does make sense to defer payments as long as is practical without risking the relationship with your supplier or your credit rating.

Better still, negotiate longer terms in the first place or, if you are really shrewd, purchase items on a consignment stock basis, which means you pay the supplier only when you sell the goods. It's not always possible or practical, but worth a try.

4. Invoice discounting and factoring

Banks have changed the way they can take security against overdrafts. They can no longer take a fixed charge against your debtor book, only a floating one. This means their security is not quite as robust as it used to be, so invoice-discounting and factoring services are more popular than ever before.

This funding option is available to most companies who provide a product or service on credit terms to customers. Its main purpose is to allow you immediate access to cash without your having to wait until your customer pays the invoice. It's a simple process and works as follows.

You issue an invoice, or for factoring the factor issues the invoice, and the funder then pays you a percentage of that invoice immediately – as much as 85 per cent in some cases. Naturally, you have to repay this when you get paid by the customer. There are terms and conditions attached to these processes, such as creditworthiness of the customer in question and debt concentration (in other words, are you overly exposed to a particular customer?).

However, for growing businesses this is a great method of funding your company. For acquirers it is also useful in that, whereas a bank is unlikely to lend in excess 50 to 60 per cent of your debtor book for a loan or overdraft, an invoice-discounting or factoring company can give you a further 30 per cent or more.

On a corporate acquisition of an existing business, sometimes this may even be extended to 100 per cent of the invoices' value for a period of time. This means that you are funding a potential deal on the value of its debtor ledger. This can be both effective and inexpensive.

Although there are some legal issues to consider, it is one of the best ways of facilitating a deal by maximising the value of the assets.

THE COST

Costs are not dissimilar in terms of the interest on the drawdown of funds from a bank overdraft, but there is also a service fee for running the facility. The two processors work essentially as follows.

Factoring
The factor (the funder) invoices and collects all your debts on your behalf so there is no need for a credit-control facility. This is usually more expensive than invoice discounting and most applicable to smaller organisations. Expect the service fee to be circa 0.5 to 3 per cent of turnover.

Invoice discounting
The funder has no direct contact with your customers, meaning you are responsible for issuing invoices and chasing the debt. Expect the service fee to be 0.1 to 1 per cent for turnover.

Facilities for both methods are often set up for 12 months or more. Check for penalties for early withdrawal and notice periods required.

5. Directors' loans

There is nothing to stop you making a personal loan to your new company if you have access to funds or can secure funds by selling or borrowing against your own assets like your house. Although it is true that funders will expect you to make a personal commitment – that's legal-speak for investing some of your own money in the company – this will usually be by way of shares. The usual commitment is about one to two years' salary per director shareholder. There may still be a need to invest further sums by way of a loan either at the start of your venture or at a later stage.

Clearly, there is a risk, since almost certainly this will have to be an unsecured loan, even if you are able to charge market interest rates (which you will have to declare for tax purposes). At best you may get some sort of subordinated security provision (that is, you will get your loan repaid after the other funders but before trade creditors, for example), but you will need to ensure you have this security registered at Companies House for it to have any real value.

6. Cash-flow lending

Often desirable but rarely granted to would-be acquirers, cash-flow lending means the funder is lending to the acquirer on the basis of future cash-flow generation – in other words, that is the only security available. From a funder's point of view, this is the least desirable option, because repayment is based on an assessment of future risk, and that's difficult and risky. So expect the funding not only hard to come by but also subject to any number of covenants in relation to the profitability, efficiency and liquidity of the business.

Be aware of the fact that banks always discount your projections by way of running a sensitivity analysis that will recognise their position on security. They will always be looking to ensure they have more than adequate headroom.

Your chances of securing a successful cash-flow loan will be greatly enhanced by the acquisition of an established company with proof of cash-flow generation. For a startup or early-stage business, the chances of this type of finance being made available are slim to nil.

7. Disposal of non-core assets

One way of funding a transaction is to sell off those assets that will no longer be required in your new company. If you are a trade acquirer and planning on amalgamating your existing company with your new one, there could be a considerable number of duplicated assets, from buildings to simple kit and equipment. Whole business divisions may be replicated.

Although you may not be able to cash in on these before the transaction, the sale of doubled-up assets could keep your working-capital requirements and thus your potential overdraft down. Always approach suitably qualified people to dispose of these assets. The last thing you want is for these to be treated as a 'fire sale'.

Commercial property that is no longer required may have an enhanced value if it can be redeveloped, so look into all angles before posting the for-sale notice with the local estate agents. One client I had was able to double the value of his secondary site by obtaining planning permission for residential development. It took a bit longer but he certainly thought the wait was worth it.

Unless they are of a specialist nature, excess plant and equipment, fixtures and fittings are unlikely to raise you vast sums. Sometimes the costs related to their sale amount to more than the sum recovered, so consider on-site auctions or even the Internet auction site eBay as your route to sale.

As for divisions, or even subsidiary businesses, you need to look at marketing these in the most effective way, but consider the possibility of an internal buyer (the management, for instance) as well as looking externally.

> ## A TIP
>
> It is of course possible to realise cash from assets that you still require in the company via a sale-and-leaseback arrangement.
>
> Particularly valuable in releasing cash is property. Commercial mortgages rarely release more than 70 to 75 per cent of value; a sale-and-leaseback to a third party such as a pension fund (internal or external) or a property developer can release 100 per cent. Clearly, you have to service the debt, and the terms of any lease will need careful thought in reference to exit choices and rent increases and so forth, but it is worth investigating.
>
> Converting your owned vehicles into a leased fleet is also a serious option and there are several specialist organisations that provide just this facility.
>
> Even a process of refunding via a revised hire-purchase agreement can release excess cash in fixtures and fittings and vehicles.
>
> Of course, you need to run your cash-flow projections to ensure you can manage interest and capital repayment, but the greatest value of this process is that it spreads the costs when in the early stages of an acquisition cash can be very tight.

Long-term routes

1. Loans

Business-loan providers abound. There are scores of them and for moderately small loans of up to £100,000 they will come up with a quick answer. Loans up to £25,000 can even be arranged online. Naturally, security is required, often your home and sometime the assets within your business. Where these are not available, personal guarantees may be required and the interest rates may sometimes approach the teens in percentage terms.

For a more structured approach you are probably better off

approaching the well-known banking providers. They are usually able to offer flexible terms and you may have a choice about whether you take fixed or variable interest-rate options, along with such alternatives as capital holidays or what are sometimes called revolving loans. Not all banks offer such a flexible approach, but, as competition in this market increases, so does choice. Here are some questions to consider.

Fixed or variable interest rate?

In other words, you agree a fixed-percentage total rate or a percentage rate above base rate. If you are a high borrower you may also want to discuss hedging your rates. This is a bit like taking a view on what rates will do over a given period, say the next five or ten years, and agreeing bands or rates that you will sit in. This is complex and worth looking at only if shifts in rates could seriously damage your business. Sometimes there are upfront costs, sometimes not, but it probably requires some help from your adviser.

Interest-only or straight repayment plan?

After your transaction, cash may be very tight, so reducing your outgoings in the early stages is worth considering. This is called a capital holiday.

What period of loan repayment do I need?

Commercial loans are usually given up to a maximum period of 20 years with a banking preference for 10 to 15. Always check you have no early-redemption penalties if you take a longer period initially, only to find you are able to accelerate this or even change funders.

Do I need all of the money right away?

You may not need all the loan in one go, so why pay interest on it? Some funders offer the opportunity to make a drawdown in tranches, called a staggered drawdown. Expect to pay for this privilege but, then, there will be an a fee in any case for each rearrangement. Check which is the more cost-effective option.

A TIP

Revolving credit

Accurately quantifying how much you need finance-wise is not always simple, so some funders are able to offer what is generally termed a revolving facility. This gives the borrower the flexibility of an overdraft in that it allows a drawdown of funds to a pre-agreed limit with a facility is in place for a longer period.

Usually, overdrafts have to be renegotiated annually. Since this revolving-credit facility could be for a number of years, be vigilant, as always, about the small print. Penalties for non-utilisation are commonplace, for instance.

Security is often required, property being favourite. Any potential shortfall in security will undoubtedly result in a requirement to fill this with a director's personal guarantee. Don't do it unless you have no option.

SMALL FIRM LOAN GUARANTEE SCHEME

In some cases where the security is simply not available, and this includes personal security, under a government-backed scheme the lender will take security from the Department of Trade and Industry (DTI), who will, subject to approval, guarantee the lender up to 75 per cent of the loan.

These funds may be available to startups or expanding businesses and can be accessed not only by limited companies but by sole traders and partnerships.

The minimum lend is £5,000 with a maximum of £250,000 (although this latter sum is available only to businesses trading for two years or more). The length of term is for between two and ten years.

►

Some business activities are excluded, including betting and gambling, commissionary agents, financial services and a few more. Nor will you be eligible if your business employs more than 200 people or turns over more than £5 million (£3 million for nonmanufacturers). Check out the DTI's website for full details.

Lenders' arrangement fees and interest rates vary between funders. This is not set by the DTI and therefore usually follows their general commercial lending criteria.

Applications require business plans in just the same way as any other loan would, including projections and sensitivities.

Don't expect a quick decision, since you are, after all, dealing with a government body – which even on the simplest application has been known to take several months.

2. Asset finance

In addition to the array of mortgage products available, ongoing capital purchases can be funded using traditional methods such as hire purchase and leases. These have different tax advantages but both allow you to utilise an asset immediately without paying out precious cash upfront.

With a hire-purchase deal you acquire eventual ownership of the asset but get tax relief only on the interest. On a leased transaction you never get ownership of the asset but get tax relief on the whole of the cost. Run this past your accountant to work out which is more valuable to you. There are lots of providers of these types of finance, so shop around for the best deal.

As an acquirer you also may have access to other unencumbered assets such as stock and work in progress (WIP). Standard bank funders attach little value to these; I even had one funder who, as part of a management buy-out, refused to lend anything against the solid silver cutlery the company manufactured, even at meltdown value.

Other types of specialist funder, however, may take a different view, taking the stock and WIP value as additional security – for instance, in an invoice-discount loan to allow 100 per cent debtor drawdown. Some very specialist funders will lend against the stock and WIP alone, although these are few in number. A million and one conditions will apply and it won't come cheap, but may be worth considering.

3. Grants

It is fairly shocking how much money is available from various grant organisations, although it's not the amount that astounds but the convoluted process of accessing it. I have come to the view in a number of cases that the money would be forthcoming only if I could prove to the provider that my client didn't need it!

One of the best places to get help is probably your local Business Link. It is possible, but not a foregone conclusion, that you will receive access to help for little or no charge, but the process is painfully slow.

Although grants sound like free money, very little comes without strings. First, you need to establish your eligibility. Some grants are designed for certain business types, others for businesses of different sizes. They may even be linked to the age of the applicant and business location.

Hardly any grants exist that provide 100 per cent of what's needed. Most are for matched funding, which means the grant provider will provide 50 per cent of the project costs as long as you fund the other 50 per cent.

Plans and projections are almost always an absolute prerequisite, so be very careful, since you could exempt yourself by mistake, in embarking on a particular project before application.

As an acquirer I would regard a grant as 'jam'. If you are wholly reliant on this making your venture work you are going to need nerves of steel and a lot of patience. Don't give up too easily, though, particularly when looking at grants for development opportunities and for startups, because you have little to lose by undertaking a full-blown investigation.

4. Vendor loans

One good way of funding your acquisition is to persuade the vendor to lend you the money. Surprisingly, this is a very common practice. In a typical situation, the acquirer (A) says to the vendor (V), 'Delighted we have a deal and have agreed the value and so on. The only problem is, I don't have sufficient funds to pay you at the moment!' But it's not necessarily 'no deal'. The vendor now has options. He can walk away disappointed and find another acquirer (not always viable) or he can say, 'OK, you have a deal. I'll lend you some of the funds to buy my business.'

Here's an example of how it might work: A gives V £2 million, the value agreed, and V gives A £500,000 back to leave in the company as a loan. To an acquirer this looks tempting but if you are the vendor it may not look so appealing. Here are a few of the issues.

Have you sorted out security?

As a matter of preference and in order of desirability, here are some options:

1. **A bank guarantee.** Essentially, this means if there is a default on the repayment plan the bank will guarantee payments. From A's point of view this is rarely available, since the funder clearly wants security before committing to guarantees.

2. **Vendor loan insurance.** Not an overpopulated market of providers in this field, but one organisation to try is Deferred Finance Limited (DFL), 13 Austin Friars, London EC2N 2JX. Restrictions exist and there is certainly no guarantee of availability. It is a risk-based decision, like any other underwriting, with a substantial cost issue – approximately 10 per cent per year of the amount deferred. However, as with the bank guarantee, from V's point of view, very appealing.

3. **Convertible-loan note.** This financial instrument allows V to take back shares (some, or all) if there is a default on the repayment plan. Complex to set up, and a vendor may not wish to take shares back from a company unable to repay its loans.

4. Unsecured. Well, this is a last-ditch effort for the vendor, really. In practice, some sort of subordinated security on residue assets in the company may be available or, if you can persuade the acquirers, a personal guarantee.

Should you be paying interest on the loan?

Realistically, the vendor will want a return on this debt – it's only reasonable – but should it be the normal lending rate, higher or lower? Loans from banks without security are rare and even when they are available they usually attract penal interest rates. Therefore, from the vendor's point of view, where no security exists, there's a good argument for a high rate.

In reality, vendor loans are often used in management buyouts where occasionally the vendor is feeling more altruistic than he might with a trade buyer, and penal rates of interest in what is already a heavily geared deal may be less acceptable to both parties. A compromise might be base lending rates plus between 1.5 and 3 per cent. If the acquirer has a good negotiator on side it may be possible to argue for base rate on the basis that it's approximately what the vendor would get in a deposit account. As with so many other entrepreneurial issues, it's about meeting halfway.

Will/should this vendor continue to have involvement in the company if they have money invested in it?

Involvement can mean different things and attracts both advantages and disadvantages. The primary benefit is that the deal can go ahead. But continuing attachment to the business might hinder the vendor's future plans and could cramp the style of the acquirer.

If the vendor has funds left in the company without security, he will want to keep up to date with financial information, management accounts, budgets and so on, and may even place covenants on management actions until the loan is repaid, such as nonapproved capital expenditure or unauthorised pay increases for the senior team.

Take a reasonable view if you want this funding option. A

nonexecutive directorship for the vendor can be an attractive sweetener to facilitate a deal.

For how long should the loan period be extended?

Periods are very variable but typically three to five years. Longer than this is usually unacceptable to both parties.

5. Deferred-contingent consideration

This method of funding a transaction is based on the premise that you don't pay for anything until you have absolute certainty of its worth. Technical valuations are to some extent based on the expectation that what's happened in the past will occur again in the future.

If only life were so certain! Businesses take a downturn (or even an upturn) for reasons that may be outside the control of the parties involved. In 2003, steel prices increased by over 60 per cent in 12 months. While UK users stocked up as much as funds would allow, prices were back to their original levels within 12 months. The impact on the profitability of those businesses with high stock levels at overvalued amounts was felt throughout most of 2004.

Issues like these can't be foreseen with any degree of confidence and therefore acquirers may want to consider how they may manage some of this risk. A deal based on a deferred-contingent consideration works like this. The acquirer has a desire to carry out the transaction but is unsure about future projections related to the business. Her doubts could be related to issues such as the security of future contracts that might be dependent on the vendor's relationships. One way of providing a greater certainty might be to suggest that a percentage of the consideration be paid when particular goals are achieved. Usually, this will mean the vendor will remain with the company in some capacity. After all, some of his future wealth is tied up with these objectives.

This raises various issues, including managing the change from being owner to being employee. The most important of all is a crystal-clear definition of the criteria to be used for the payment. I have seen thousands of pounds – in fact tens of thousands of pounds – whittled away during arguments about whether or not the profit levels agreed as the baseline trigger for payments were correct.

Also, keep the time periods for the deferred payments to a minimum. Extended periods rarely work for either party.

6. Equity

I have deliberately left this controversial funding source until the latter part of this section. Many entrepreneurs I have worked with have lived to regret involving equity players in their business – but it is fair to say too that the same people probably couldn't have gone ahead with the transaction in the first place without equity funding.

The trick in dealing with equity funders is to choose the player cautiously. If you have an exciting deal, equity players will be fighting to get to the front of the queue so they can get a slice of the business. However, unlike the case with some products, they don't always do what they say on the tin. Look carefully at the small print and ensure you can build a relationship with the individuals with whom you will have most contact after completion.

Smaller-scale transactions involving equity sums below £1 million will be of no interest to most mainstream players but there are local and regional funders who will pick up these opportunities. Deals in tens of thousands of pounds usually attract angel funding. Where your deal is £3 million-plus, funding options for equity become wider. Start talking £10 million plus and they abound.

I am sure you see the immediate funding-gap problems. There is no easy answer, sadly, but I keep lobbying. This is where vendor loans tend to raise their head as an option.

For 95 per cent of equity funders of whatever nature, the big money-making opportunity is on exit, so your business is unlikely to be of much interest if this opportunity seems unlikely within three to five years. Indeed, some funders have absolute limits on investment periods because of how they draw down funds from their own investors, be they European funds or government funds.

Return requirements are high: 35 to 40 per cent per year would not be an unusual stipulation. Remember that, by and large, these funders are investing from a wholly unsecured position (but don't feel too sorry for them) and therefore must make this sort of premium to compensate for those deals which fail, and lots do!

Funds are invested in various ways: wholly equity, for instance, a share stake (and these can be ordinary shares or shares with preferential rights attached to them such as dividend or voting rights) or convertible loans (loans that convert to equity on exit). And there can be a mix of all these.

With the vast majority of funding comes the stipulation that the funder should have a nominee director on the board to represent his interests. The post is usually paid for by the company rather than the funder, so try to influence candidate selection – or even choose your own.

Selling equity in a transaction is an emotional process for the acquirer. The returns seem to be, well, inequitable! And why is it necessary to have a nominee director on the board issuing orders? The fact is, without this type of finance, a deal may not be possible at all, so it's simply a question of negotiating hard on the terms and taking a pragmatic view on the outcome.

Look at investment agreements carefully, both conditions pre-deal and post-deal (known as precedent and subsequent). Have a well-drawn-up shareholders' agreement and discuss openly their secondary investment criteria. You may need more development funding or, in a worst-case scenario, rescue financing.

The British Venture Capital Association (BVCA) is a good source of reference and, for angel groups and local funding, speak to your local Business Link as a first step. Your corporate finance advisers will have lots of contacts and will also know who is doing deals and who isn't.

Some main criteria issues for these kinds of funder are:

- industry type;

- deal size;

- stage of business development (disregard pre-revenue – that is, pre-sales – or startup; only a very small number of providers exist);

- quality and ambition of the management team;

- growth and expansion opportunities;

- quality of customers' suppliers and contracts;

- IP protection.

A TIP

Expect to have to invest approximately two years of your salary in a deal backed by an equity investor.

---

7. Mezzanine finance

Intentionally left until last, mezzanine finance is neither debt nor equity but an interim product. Think of it as a kind of bridging loan. When all sources of available funding have been explored and a gap remains, mezzanine funders can come into play.

This finance, attracting returns similar to equity but appearing like debt in the balance sheet, is usually placed for only short periods – one or two years maximum. Defaults on payments may result in conversion options, such as the right to change the debt into equity, which dilutes management equity. The costs and these seemingly onerous rights tend to encourage acquirers to remove this finance from the balance sheet as soon as possible. Specialist funders exist for this at both national and regional levels, with some high street banks dipping a toe into the market.

Chain of events for raising finance

Elements of this depend on the nature of the transaction. This assumes the requirement is development funding.

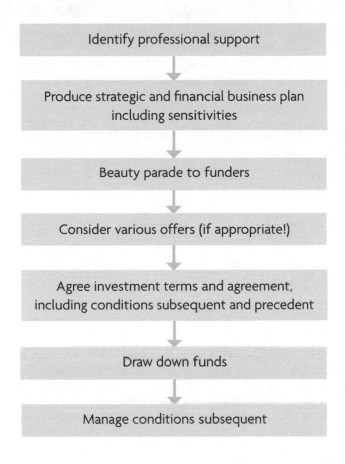

Identify professional support

↓

Produce strategic and financial business plan including sensitivities

↓

Beauty parade to funders

↓

Consider various offers (if appropriate!)

↓

Agree investment terms and agreement, including conditions subsequent and precedent

↓

Draw down funds

↓

Manage conditions subsequent

What funders want from you

Without question, different funders want various things, but these are some of the most obvious. Whatever type of funder you are dealing with it goes without saying that all providers want you to have clear objectives about what the money required is for and how you plan to give them their expected return on the investment. I have seen countless plans where not only are the objectives obscure but the actual amount of funding required is not even quantified.

In any request for funding, be sure to clarify both issues up-front, with as much definition as possible. While there is lots of funding available, this is more than matched by the number of requests for financial aid, many of which are totally unrealistic.

State your case, its rationale, your planned use of the finance and exactly how much and when you need it. For example, you may wish to draw down funds in tranches rather than in one lump. Set benchmark criteria that can be succinctly measured to indicate why and how you will police your performance.

THE APPROACH

It's always vital to make a good first impression, never more so than when seeking funding. You have only one chance to do that.

The most successful approach is likely to be made via a professional whom the funders know and respect. The number of applications for funding is substantial, with many attempts being unrealistic. Funders have limited time and therefore may pay less heed to a proposition received from an unknown source.

Arrange a face-to-face meeting as quickly as possible and don't be afraid to sell yourself. It is you and your team that funders are investing in as much as the business.

Try to find out beforehand their preferred style. Do they

want an all-singing, all-dancing PowerPoint presentation round a boardroom table with everyone suited and booted? Or a more casual approach with a coffee table chat? Don't be fooled by the latter: it is just as serious, but less formal.

I find virgin entrepreneurs are more comfortable in their own environment, but some funders will expect you to visit them. If you do have a choice, pick somewhere you feel most relaxed.

Take your team and ensure they are all well briefed. One person needs to lead the discussion, but technical questions (if there are any at this early stage) need expert answers. If you are at all concerned about this, run a dress rehearsal with your adviser.

Funders are, by and large, experienced negotiators and will expect a degree of skill from you in this area. Your corporate-finance adviser will be able to handle this, but you cannot abdicate responsibility.

They will soon want to hear about your absolute commitment to the process and this means both emotional and financial. If they want you to jump, ask how high!

Always anticipate problems – deals are fraught with them and the funding agreement has no fewer than any other element.

Establish in your preliminary discussions any crucial issues that need addressing before you progress.

Some banks promise the world in initial discussions, leaving the acquirer in disbelief when the credit committee turns down the request. So remain guarded in your expectations.

Finally, agree timetables for progress and make it clear this funder isn't your only option (even if it is). And yet be cautious if you indulge in brinkmanship, since you don't want to shoot the only horse in the race.

All funders require financial due diligence of some sort. They test your assumptions and run sensitivities on your projections. They also verify historical statements about the financial performance of the business.

The funder is in effect looking at the level of risk. Many debt funders appear to be super-cautious; but consider the positives of this exercise, because detailed intervention like this may reveal issues you have overlooked. Either way, the outcome of this exercise, in most cases, is a deciding factor in whether the funds can be drawn down.

A detailed plan and projections are also a requisite for most lenders. Its extent varies with the substance of the funds required but, suffice it to say, the most important part certainly in the early stages, is the executive summary. This is in effect a synopsis of the whole plan. Three to four pages is probably about the right length to detail those salient facts – think clarity and brevity.

However, substance is important for the body of the plan. As well as the rationale, market, personnel and operations, the financial plan needs to be robust and thoroughly tested by 'what-ifs'. You will need three years' worth of forecasts showing a month-by-month summary. As a minimum, look at a profit-and-loss account, cash flow and balance sheet. Clearly, the further into the future you look, the less specific you can be; but bear in mind that banks always discount such figures, so give yourself some realistic leeway.

Don't forget to include the financial assumptions you have used and summarise your capital-expenditure plans as a separate schedule.

Ninety-nine per cent of all plans I review in the early stages show a 'hockey stick' performance curve. It never happens – oh, OK, it rarely happens! It is fine to be cautiously optimistic but, above all, be realistic.

Most companies rely to a substantial degree on the competency and skills of the management team. Funders are attuned to this particular factor. In an ideal funding proposition they need evidence of a comprehensive team, which means having a key member in each crucial area – finance, sales operations, technical logistics – and, of course, a team leader. These comfort factors are further enhanced by your own financial commitment. In a buy-in without equity funding, expect to commit about one year's salary, with equity funding about two years' salary. As a matter of course, equity funders tend to check out the management team's credentials, credit rating and history. Any copybook blots need to be revealed early with the relevant explanations.

A deal I nearly didn't complete came to a painfully abrupt halt when the funders discovered that one of the buy-in team had an undisclosed County Court judgment (CCJ) against him.

The ongoing quality of management information is pretty important to the funding world. After all, if you can't monitor your performance with an acceptable degree of speed and accuracy, what hope have the funders in taking remedial action before possible disaster strikes?

Some funders will want to take a proactive role in determining both availability of this information and its production. Others may be satisfied with receiving the stated data on schedule along with attendance at occasional debriefing meetings. Minimal levels of information usually include monthly management accounts, budgets and projections and some monitoring of key performance indicators such as debtors' days and gross profit. This provides the funder with some degree of **confidence in your ability to make payments scheduled**, whether that be interest payments, loan redemptions or dividends.

Don't forget that a bank is in business to make a return on its investment and, if there is any doubt about your ability to adhere to these requirements, the bank's first job is to minimise its exposure.

THE RIGHT BANK

One deal with a management buy-out was especially tough. The bank involved was particularly difficult as it changed terms throughout. Shortly before completion, having previously agreed to an unsecured loan, the bank team made new demands and the whole deal came to a stop. Without prior warning

▶

everyone in the management team had put up their home as security.

As the deal was once more poised to complete, the bank came back with another fresh condition. This time it dictated that, if the team changed banks within five years, there would be a £40,000 exit fee.

The bank in question was using the Leeds office of a legal firm while the venture capitalists were using a different office of the same firm. For no apparent reason, the bank stopped negotiations between the lawyers until everything had been scrutinised by themselves.

Then, on the point of completion with the fees for all parties agreed, the bank insisted completion would not go ahead unless everyone agreed a 30 per cent reduction in fees. By now everyone was ready to agree to anything to get the deal done. The first date for completion was December. After that it was on and off more times than I care to remember. It finally occurred in August after I notched up a £500 mobile-phone bill on my summer holiday in Cyprus. Needless to say, I have never worked with that bank again.

When you are negotiating on repayment plans, first think carefully about capital-holiday plans (a capital holiday is a period during a loan-repayment programme when only interest is paid), particularly in the early stages of an investment.

The **utilisation of financial covenants** gives the bank funders the opportunity to exercise a degree of contractual control over you for breaching such requirements.

Covenants can be precedential ones (those agreements that must be complied with prior to drawing down of the funds such as an acceptable valuation on a property). Or they can be conditions subsequent that must be managed after the funds are drawn down and that, if they are breached, afford the funder any number of rights, including the right to withdraw the funding completely.

While these issues are common to all funding types by and large, some requirements are unique to different funders. For debt funders, the two critical issues are the ability to service the debt (that is, maintain interest payments) and the security available if the funder needs to access the capital in advance of Plan A. This means the value of the assets they lend against is of crucial importance along with the level of profit the business is generating before it has to pay earnings before interest and tax (EBIT).

With regard to security within asset value the following would be a typical view taken by many high street funders.

Buildings	up to 75% of market value.
Debtors	up to 50% of debt under 90 days old. This can be increased substantially if an invoice-discounting or factoring facility is used.
Fixtures and fittings	10% of book value if you are lucky. It's usually nothing at all.
Plant and equipment	Dependent on what it is, a specialist funder can go as much as 50–60% of value but a high street bank is unlikely to attach anything other than a notional value to these types of asset.
Investments	For investments held in nonlisted businesses, this is dependent on the investment percentage, but banks rarely lend against shares in other private businesses due to the difficulty in realising worth. Investments in listed companies may attract a value but a very cautious approach will be taken.
Goodwill	Good luck! Usually nothing at all unless you can quantify this against something a little more tangible, such as a patent that may have a resale value.

As far as servicing the debt is concerned, the debt funder is looking to ensure that the interest owed can be easily generated from the profits of the company. Most banks look for three times plus operating profit over interest payable. To prop up possible differences in their requirements, banks often seek personal guarantees from the acquirer. Rarely are buyers inclined towards this particular option, but without it you may become the deal breaker.

If it's a must-have from the funder's point of view, at least manage your own risk, by signing only a several guarantee rather than a joint-and-several. By way of explanation, this makes you liable only for your element of the outstanding debt; a joint-and-several guarantee leaves you exposed to the whole of the due debt.

Look for time limits, since this way you can at least have the opportunity to revisit the guarantee annually with the funder, who is often reluctant to give the guarantee back. Limit the guarantee in amount. Unlimited personal guarantees leave you exposed to personal ruin. Finally, remember no personal guarantee is binding unless your domestic partner has taken separate legal advice about its implications in relation to any jointly owned assets, in particular the primary residence.

From an equity investor's view point, security is less of an issue. After all, this is meant to be risk capital.

So what do these investors want? Primarily, they seek a return on their investment, which is generally realised by leaving the company with a premium on the sale of shares. This exit route generally needs to be in the foreseeable future, so think three to five years. Any plans wanting to attract this sort of investment need to clarify how this result will be achieved, the obvious route being trade sale, floating or refinancing via an MBO, for instance. It's difficult to secure terms for anything going beyond that. Also, these types of investor almost always want some involvement in the direction of the business and will often, via a nominee, take a seat on the board.

CHAPTER 9

Due Diligence and Completion

THEY SAY NO PAIN, no gain! Well, this is the painful part of the process, when what seemed like a dream deal may become a nightmare.

Due diligence is the process whereby the acquirer or the funders investigate the business in question to satisfy themselves about its value and to discover whether there are any hidden nasties. It is usually carried out after the 'subject to' commitment is made by the funders/investors. These processes cover a variety of areas, depending on the industry involved and the complexity of the deal.

The examination process can be in minute detail, looking at all sides of the organisation, including you and your fellow directors. Some processes are structured and formatted, others less so, depending on the view of the investor. It can be time-consuming and debilitating as well as expensive. This is a cost you will have to bear in most cases, whether or not your deal completes, so be prepared. The extent of the process is variable, partly due to the perceived risk by the investor and sometimes because of market conditions.

Commercial due diligence

This will be carried out by your own advisers or even you, and will assess business issues in relation to the transaction. If you use outside help for this, there will be a cost.

Financial due diligence

Unless you are investing only your own funds, this will be carried out by professionals appointed by the investor. The areas under scrutiny include:

- the structure of the business;

- its financial strength;

- its longer-term prospects;

- a sensitivity analysis on your plans;

- the integrity and trustworthiness of you and your team.

Legal due diligence

This process involves the lawyers checking that the company does not have any significant legal problems. Potentially, any documents could be examined but here are the usual ones you would expect them to check:

- contracts of employment;

- key contracts with suppliers and customers;

- NDA with employees past and present;

- articles of association;

- shareholders' agreement;

- any litigation documents;

- contingent liabilities that may have a litigious element;

- any minutes or consents needed from the board or the share-holders;

- any documents relating to IP.

Other due-diligence areas that may be required include environmental, technical, HR, product and market. Where specialist or innovative products and services are being used or when investors feel particularly vulnerable, these can form significant parts of the process. Specialists will be employed, who are usually costly.

My advice is to be pragmatic about this process. Even if this activity turns up something undesirable that culminates in a re-think of the deal or even its failure, it must surely be better to have prior knowledge than to go ahead on a wobbly footing.

I had one deal where the due-diligence process revealed a dishonest vendor who fraudulently claimed certain company assets that didn't belong to him. The revelations caused my client to withdraw from negotiations. However, six months later, when the business in question collapsed, he was able to negotiate a speedy deal with the liquidators.

YOUR COMPLETION CHECKLIST

Crack open the champagne, toll the bells, dance on the tables! Well, not yet. Completion for the acquirer is only the start of a long process – this is when the hard work usually starts.

But I definitely don't want to be a killjoy, as there is usually a real sense of achievement along with relief and satisfaction when this day eventually dawns.

I can almost guarantee the agreed date will have been delayed, not once but probably several times. You are bound to have seen several false summits but, if this is the day Everest is conquered, then this is what is likely to happen.

Usually completion meetings are held in your lawyer's office.

▶

My advice is start early, as they will inevitably drag on often long into the night and sometimes into the next day.

Your lawyers will have a checklist of the process as follows.

1. Pre-completion

1.1 Consents/approvals available from, for example:
   a) shareholders;
   b) completion authorities;
   c) licensing authorities;
   d) landlords;
   e) lenders;
   f) contracting parties.

1.2 Tax clearances available.

1.3 Bankruptcy/company/winding-up searches clear and up to date.

1.4 Any presale reorganisation/transfer of assets completed.

1.5 Disclosure bundles prepared and verified.

1.6 Lists of included/excluded assets and liabilities finalised.

1.7 Property services clear and up to date.

1.8 Trademark/patent services clear and up to date.

1.9 Conditions precedent satisfied/waived.

1.10 Employees consulted/informed.

1.11 Insurance arrangements in place.

1.12 Buyer board meeting.

1.13 Seller board meeting.

1.14 Powers of attorney executed.

1.15 Foreign legal opinions finalised.

1.16 Business bank statements and reconciliations verified.

1.17 Press/staff/customer/supplier announcements agreed.

1.18 Due-diligence reports finalised.

1.19 Arrangements in place for delivery/possession at completion of relevant assets, contracts, records and other documents.

▶

2. Post-completion

2.1 Stamp duty paid.

2.2 Completion accounts prepared and agreed and outstanding consideration settled.

2.3 Any outstanding contracts novated.

2.4 Notifications to customers/suppliers/employees delivered.

2.5 Assignments/transfers of IP and real property registered.

2.6 Charges registered.

2.7 Statutory forms filed at Companies House.

2.8 New pension-scheme arrangements.

2.9 New VAT registrations.

2.10 Transaction bibles prepared and circulated.

As you work your way through this enormous process with your lawyers, you will be signing one document after another, the ultimate effect of which is to transfer the business or the assets to you, the new owner.

Of course, it is rare for it to be all plain sailing. All sorts of issues have been raised at the numerous completions I have attended, including:

- company seals going missing;

- vendors losing certificates;

- contingent liabilities suddenly crystallising;

- worst of all, a vendor dying at the meeting – too horrific to recollect!

At times like these you need to keep calm and rely on the skills of your advisers to deal with last-minute hitches. After all, that is what you are paying them for.

A final checklist for the buyer

Along with all the items mentioned at the end of Chapter 6 (information required for valuations) and the vital information section, you should also see as a minimum, if possible before committing ultimately to the transaction, the following:

- investment agreements with banks and other funders;
- strategy documents;
- key policy documents such as health-and-safety, risk and environmental;
- board meeting minutes for last three years;
- information on key products and services, personnel and so on;
- statutory books and records;
- shareholders' agreement;
- employee files and records;
- insurance policies;
- VAT and other Revenue and Customs information;
- supplier agreements with particular reference to retrospective rebates, cancellation policies and exclusivity issues.

Or you could try a mystery shopping trip.

PART **3**

Selling

Chain of events for a typical sale

As with the buying flow chart we saw at the beginning of Part 2, some areas run concurrently.

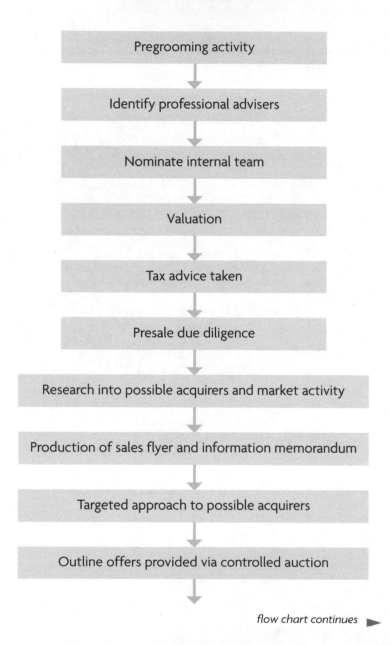

Pregrooming activity

Identify professional advisers

Nominate internal team

Valuation

Tax advice taken

Presale due diligence

Research into possible acquirers and market activity

Production of sales flyer and information memorandum

Targeted approach to possible acquirers

Outline offers provided via controlled auction

flow chart continues ▶

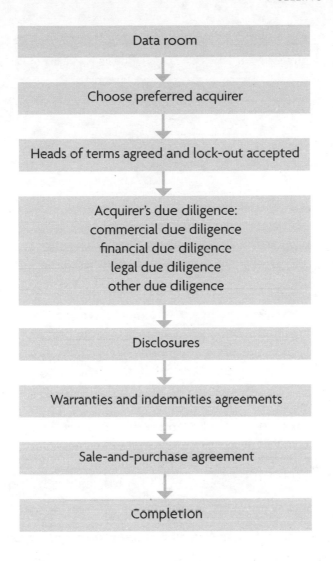

CHAPTER **10**

Is it Time to Sell?

SELLING WHEN YOU WANT to is clearly the most advantageous, but this is not an activity that should be entered into lightly. It is a time-consuming and arduous process and so planning is essential. There are a myriad reasons why entrepreneurs decide to put their business up for sale. You may be considering retirement or just be bored or dissatisfied with the whole enterprise. Or it could be that the business is no longer profitable and you don't want to invest further in a venture in which you've lost faith.

Whatever the reason, planning and timing will help you achieve a more favourable deal. It's key to avoiding the elephant trap of appearing desperate to sell.

Expect the transaction to take, on average, 6–12 months. Of course, some transactions are a lot quicker and a few longer, but this is a norm. Don't forget that throughout the whole process you also have your 'day job', that is keeping the business going and maintaining or improving profits. Any downturn will almost always affect value adversely.

There are always tens of thousands of businesses for sale at any one time, not all of them saleable. The state of the economy, as well as your own business performance, has an effect. Even fashion trends can influence the timing of a sale. If you are considering a sale, keep an eye on these external factors. Issues such as falling rates of interest and positive trends in your market can create that important catalyst.

Presale grooming

Before selling your home, you will probably consider spring cleaning or even decorating to bring it to its best. Preparing your business for sale requires the same process, called grooming. The aim of presale grooming is to get both your business and yourself into tip-top condition to ensure you sell at maximum value.

This means looking at issues that may reduce value and putting them right. This might include updating poorly presented or inadequate information, improving your business environment and the quality of your facilities, and enhancing all those positives in the organisation such as registration of IP and quality of staff training.

Grooming also includes looking at your most effective tax opportunities. These need clarifying before you embark on any sale process (see Chapter 13).

YOUR PRESALE CHECKLIST

In addition to a tax overhaul and the essential tidy-up, here is a list of information you should start to gather together and take action on as necessary:

- statutory books, including shareholder details;

- incorporation certificates;

- articles of association;

- shareholders' agreements;

- audited accounts for the last three years;

- details of overdraft arrangements and other loans;

▶

- completed tax returns and any relevant correspondence with Revenue and Customs;
- all agreements relating to major customers and suppliers;
- all standard terms of business;
- all insurance policies and details of any claims made within the past five years;
- list of properties owned or occupied with details of use, ownership, rateable value, mortgages and sublettings, including copies of leases;
- asset register;
- details of patents, trademarks, registered designs and copyrights and disputes that may exist;
- all licences, or consents in relation to the business or premises;
- any environmental audit carried out at any premises used or owned by the business;
- current health-and-safety policy and the last safety audit;
- organisation chart;
- employee contracts;
- all other agreements with employees relating to benefits and share options;
- standard terms and conditions together with any employee handbook;
- details of any company pension arrangements or schemes in place, together with list of employees participating in them;
- details of any existing, pending or threatened arbitration or litigation together with amounts involved.

This is not a comprehensive list but it's certainly a start.

The more detailed and up to date your information, the better placed you will be for negotiations that result in a credible offer. Hiding critical information for fear that it will adversely affect the value is simply a nonstarter.

In smaller organisations, owner-managers are often seduced by the idea of reducing tax year on year. Trouble is, this is almost certainly going to reduce the value of your business if you have burdensome overheads in an effort to reduce taxable profits.

Hence the whole point of grooming for sale is to start early and eliminate bogeys like this. In an ideal world you need steady or increasing profits for a minimum of three years. In the meantime, you may have to pay more tax but hopefully there will be compensation through the increased value you will achieve on sale.

As most people sell only one business in a lifetime, you need to ensure the grooming process is thorough and focused. That's also how you must be during the ensuing sale.

PREPARE YOURSELF

Vendors will make a number of mistakes throughout this arduous time so here are a few issues to take on board.

- Don't attempt to sell your organisation without outside help. Unless your business is tiny, this is false economy. Astute acquirers will always use professionals and without someone on your side they will outsmart you on one or more issues.

- Get all your information and business systems in shape before you start the process. This helps towards realistic negotiations and speeds up the whole process.

- Be realistic in terms of both value and time. In other words, ask yourself whether you would pay your chosen price to buy the business. If not, you are possibly starting from an unrealistic position.

▶

- You are unlikely to achieve all the value on Day One. More and more deals are based on some sort of deferment, so if you dismiss this as an option, you lose a whole raft of acquirers.

- Don't put a price tag on your business, unless it's a very modest business indeed. The best way is to solicit offers, since you may get a pleasant surprise with an offer in excess of your expectations.

- Don't underestimate how draining this will be. The sheer volume of paperwork, never mind the countless meetings with advisers and acquirers, is often debilitating.

CHAPTER **11**

What Are You Selling?

The process

When you come to the sale process each particular transaction has its own nuance. These depend not only on the size of the deal in question but also on the industry and the personalities of the parties involved. At the beginning of Part 3 you will find a flowchart called 'Chain of events for a typical sale', which shows the approximate events involved in the sale process, but it might not happen that way. Stumbles and restarts are commonplace.

Once you are surrounded by the appropriate advisers, internal and external, and have taken part in the tax grooming process, these are some of the activities that are likely to occur.

1. Creating your company's information memorandum

It is possible to sell some companies without an information memorandum (IM), but for an average-sized business it is highly recommended. This document provides a detailed description of the organisation you are presenting for sale. Getting the content of this pitched correctly in terms of detail and volume is an art form.

Too much and it is boring and may even impart confidential information too soon. If it is too brief you will be besieged with requests for additional data – or potential acquirers will be left cold by what's in front of them and 'won't bite'.

I describe an IM as a little like a CV for a prospective employer. Its content ensures your target acquirers are sufficiently interested to meet you but there's enough additional information to garner further interest during a face-to-face meeting.

Your corporate-finance team will probably write most of this for you, using your input of course. Although the detailed content will be specific to your business the following areas should typically be covered.

- **Executive summary.** A few pages to summarise the content within the memorandum.

- **Your company information.** This should cover your rationale for selling. Write this with care and include a brief history of the business and reasons why it is successful.

- **The industry.** Provide an overview of the industry and its future potential, your market share and a competitor analysis.

- **Your products/service.** This is a breakdown of your products and services and their contributions to revenue and profit, how you market them and any new developments pending.

- **Customers and suppliers.** An overview of the type of customers and suppliers you have and a percentage breakdown of trade. While no names are needed, it is worth stating whether they are blue-chip. It is also worthwhile detailing any contracts in existence.

- **Personnel.** An organisation chart and a profile of key staff. (No names are needed.)

- **Asset details.** If you have an asset register, submit this along with your depreciation policy. Critical assets such as buildings can be photographed.

- **Plans.** A brief summary of potential income generation is all that is needed.

- **Financial statements.** Three years' audited accounts and up-to-date management accounts are usual.

- **Appendix.** This can include, for example, photographs, marketing information, leases, detailed CVs, product catalogues.

The most important section is the executive summary, so make it sharp, clear and persuasive. Use colour and photographs and lots of white space and wide margins.

If possible email your IM rather than use snail mail. Not only is it immediate but lots of institutional investors need to copy this to various committees and it is much easier to do so if it is accessible electronically.

2. Creating the flyer

This single-page summary of your business details the salient points contained within the IM. However, it does not mention the company name or its location. This is used to solicit initial enquiries from potential acquirers.

INFORMATION REQUIRED FOR AN INFORMATION MEMORANDUM

Information questionnaire

1. History and ownership

Key developments in the business and dates.

Current and historic ownership structure.

Markets served, dates and reasons of moves into or out of key markets.

Any significant change in operations, reasons/strategy.

Details of any business acquisitions or disposals.

Details of international operations.

▶

Details of formation and activities of any related limited companies (dates, reasons for founding company, directors and so forth).

2. Financial information

Full company and subsidiary accounts for the three years to the last accounts date.

Reasons for major movements in turnover, gross profit and administrative expenses.

Details of any one-off/unusual costs in these figures.

Latest management accounts for the period since last audited accounts (if available).

Detailed financial projections for the current year (if available).

3. Nature of operations and suppliers

Details of typical project, size and procedure.

Details of current contracts.

Overview of the operations of each department of the company (purchasing, manufacturing, stockholding, distribution, sales and marketing).

Relationships and standard terms of trade/contracts with major suppliers.

Details of major supplier contracts.

Computer systems and development.

Marketing team's organisation, strategy (if applicable).

Copies of all recent promotional material and product catalogues.

Ownership of any IP rights and ongoing costs and litigation.

Quality and other industry accreditations.

▶

4. Premises and equipment

Particulars of premises (area, usage, rental, cost).

Terms of any leases.

Size of the premises and current level of capacity.

Details of major/high-value capital equipment.

Revaluations of any equipment.

5. Markets, competitors and customers

Market overview, structure and size.

Any market reports and surveys whether internal or external.

Key competitors (public and private) in the markets served.

Price, service and quality competitiveness.

Analysis of customer base – sales quantum, geographic split, product types.

Proportion of income from top customers.

Details of major customer contracts and history of relationship.

6. Management, organisation and control

6.1 Directors and key staff for each department.

Age.

Qualifications.

Experience and length of service.

Role within business.

Strengths of second-tier management.

Overview CVs of key staff.

▶

6.2 Other staff

Standard and any unusual working hours, holiday allowances, bonus schemes, incentives and so on.

Subcontractor arrangements.

Pension schemes.

Organisation charts to include numbers in each department.

Trade union involvement of staff and recognition (if any).

7. Future developments

Strategy and goals of the business.

Current new projects and associated costs.

Potential new markets.

Technological development in existing markets (if applicable).

Any outstanding litigation or potential liabilities.

8. Other key selling points

Any other key marketable aspects of the company.

Notable successes.

Favourable press comment.

3. Targeting the acquirer

There are likely to be any number of people who will want to acquire your business. The trouble is finding them. If you are selling your house, the process is straightforward. You put a sign outside and an advert in the newspaper, or the property appears in an estate agent's window. For smaller businesses, any one of these techniques may work, but for something a little more substantial this is an inappropriate way of accessing your market.

Rainmakers and corporate financiers along with bankers and lawyers will have a much better approach tailored for larger enterprises. Not only do they have access to serial entrepreneurs and corporates actively looking for transactions but their skills in brokering the deal while maintaining confidentiality is probably better than an 'own sale' in most cases.

You may consider promoting your business on the various websites (see Appendix 2) that advertise businesses for sale. This is cost-effective and of course potentially reaches a global audience, but my experience is that this is a last-ditch process for many vendors, with most deals of any substance being completed without taking this path.

4. Determining eligibility

Of course lots of organisations and people may say they want to buy your business, but it is entirely possible they have neither the will nor the wherewithal to do so. These are what we term fishermen, people with no intention at all in buying the company but, as a competitor, with a vested interest in finding out more about your business.

Corporate financiers should qualify any prospective buyer before issuing them with the IM but, if this has not been carried out, there are some areas you will need to investigate. Clearly, you will know if the prospective purchaser is from your industry – and many potential acquirers are likely to be. In this case you don't need to know who they are, but whether they are genuine.

This could be proved by previous industry acquisitions. There may be published information recording a desire to acquire – for instance, a business plan, board minutes. You may even demand an abort fee from a serious trade rival. It means that, if they withdraw from negotiations for undisclosed or unacceptable reasons, they forfeit a fee. This is difficult to negotiate but sends the right signals to nosey opponents.

Funding a deal is a major concern to many vendors and, although funding can come from various sources, including the vendor, one qualification often required is proof about financing.

For reputable companies of blue-chip status, this is less relevant than to an MBI candidate or a small corporate. However, you should always seek evidence from appropriate funders about their willingness to support a transaction under certain prespecified conditions.

You need to feel pretty comfortable with the capabilities of the new owners, especially if payment to you has been deferred. Ask yourself what experience they have in this sector and whether their culture is likely to be compatible with your own. If you are unable to qualify or quantify any of the information requirements, you need to think carefully about whether to proceed, since you could be embarking on a long walk down a short path.

5. Issuing the confidentiality agreement and IM

Having established the identity of the likely buyers (detailed in the next chapter), the next stage of the process is to issue them with the flyer and a nondisclosure agreement (an NDA – sometime also known as a confidentiality agreement), which they will sign and complete before receiving the full information memorandum.

This furnishes you with a legally binding agreement through which you can take action if the potential acquirer misuses the data they receive through the IM regarding your company.

Once the NDA is returned, the process of issuing the full IM can commence. The IMs should be numbered so they can be tracked. Always ask acquirers to return them should they decide not to proceed to the next stage.

Attach a covering letter to the IM restating contact details and agreeing deadlines for initial offers. Always make it clear that initial offers should confirm ability to finance the purchase debt, including support letters from a bank where relevant. Although your IM will have provided a deadline date for offers, you may also want to restate this in your covering letter and advise possible acquirers that they can make contact to clarify any points they may wish to discuss.

About two weeks before the deadline date ring round the recipients of the IM to assess just who is likely to be making offers.

DATA ROOMS

This element of the transaction is not necessarily relevant to every deal but, with multiple bidders, it is useful for firming up the initial offers.

Initial offers received after the issuing of the IM are just that. They do not constitute final offers, since at this stage the acquirer has not completed any formal due diligence.

So a data room provides an arena for progress. It's a facility in which a certain amount of controlled data (more extensive than that contained in the IM but without highly sensitive information such as customer names) can be given to the would-be acquirer.

Usually set up off site, at the offices of your lawyer or corporate financier, it is accessed by the acquiring team or their advisers. This gives them the opportunity to explore issues further with the aim of firming up an initial offer, changing it or withdrawing.

At this stage the vendor will not have given any party an exclusive advantage. A shrewd vendor makes sure the acquirer knows this and the fact that there are a number of other interested parties (even when these are few and far between).

By now a time frame dictates the progress of the sale. Having had access to the data room, the would-be bidder must firm up on their offer and indicate their terms in a little more detail.

As a vendor, if you like what you hear you will hopefully be in the happy position of providing an exclusivity period to a chosen acquirer, who, incidentally, may not be the highest bidder.

Providing an exclusivity period or lock-out does not mean excluding the other bidders permanently. Clearly, this delicate stage needs careful handling, since your chosen bidder may not be the ultimate acquirer. On several occasions I have had to resort to a second choice when the original bidder backed out later in the proceedings.

6. Negotiation

The ensuing negotiations are time-consuming and can be traumatic. My advice is to meet face to face as soon as possible and to take your advisers with you so you can play 'good cop' to their 'bad cop'. This will be a smoother procedure if you have been honest in your business presentation rather than if you have either glossed over or hidden some important fact. I have seen deals fall away swiftly upon the discovery of some real 'nasties', such as underfunded pension schemes and nontransferable contracts.

You may also discover that you have encountered some time wasters who just want a closer look at your company – and there are plenty of these about. A good corporate financier should have sniffed these out long before they come to the negotiating table but it's a fact of life that some slip through the net.

While everything is for sale at a price, you will have a walkaway value in mind – or at least you should have. This is the offer that's simply too low to take. Sometimes a miserly offer has incentives in the way it is structured, so remain flexible and take advice from your corporate financier.

7. Heads of terms

Once the deal in principle is agreed, formal heads of terms will be signed. These give an outline of the transaction and the terms attached to it. Other than a couple of terms such as the lock-out period and the exclusivity period, they are not binding, but they are the essence of the deal and need to be crystal clear, since it is from this that the sale-and-purchase agreement will be drawn up.

8. Due diligence

In addition to the professional and financial process, it is possible that the potential acquirer will want to see your business site and even talk to your key staff. He will certainly anticipate a premises visit, even if it's out of office hours.

Proceed with care, since you do not have a deal yet. On the other hand, if you don't comply with requests for a tour you could look suspicious. Use common sense and brief carefully any staff who become involved. While I usually warn against early meetings with key management, it is sometimes a critical element in a deal, particularly in a BIMBO or private equity transaction. Take advice from your corporate financier, who will be able to recommend how you proceed.

9. Renegotiation

There will inevitably be lots of this. Usually it's as a result of the due-diligence process and nine times out of ten it's down to acquirers looking for reasons as to why the value now attached to the deal is less than originally thought.

In the first instance leave negotiation to your advisers, provided they are well instructed and they know the parameters of the deal. They should not go outside those areas without your consent. Using an intermediary leaves a door open to you for intervention should the transaction start to go awry.

In negotiation you have a clear advantage where you have other potential acquirers on the horizon. If you are not in this fortunate position you need to bear in mind the possibility of walking away. Keep talking within an agreed time frame. It is all simply a case of holding your nerves, particularly if the other side indulge in brinkmanship.

10. Sale-and-purchase agreement

It's the start of the completion process and this agreement can run to several hundred pages. Prepared by the acquirer's solicitors in most cases, it details in full what the business will be sold for, how and when payments will be made and where and when the transaction will take place. It will also contain any loan and asset documents and agreements.

It is this document that will 'wing' backwards and forwards between the acquirer's lawyers and your own scores of times before it is finally agreed weeks or months later. At completion this document is signed by both parties and initiates the official handover of the business (subject to funding being in place of course).

Critical within this are the warranties and indemnities you provide for your acquirer. There will be more wringing of hands and thumping of tables during this part of the process than you can believe possible.

11. Finally ...

Make a will and keep it up to date. Vendors should always make a will to ensure that assets are distributed as they desire and as tax-efficiently as possible. Also, put life insurance in place to cover any inheritance tax (IHT) liability. This will need to be written in a suitable form of trust so that it does not fall into your estate for tax purposes. If not, the insurance money will be taxed along with the rest of the estate.

SHARES VERSUS ASSETS – EQUITY RELEASE

If you have read Part 2 of this book, you will know that in buying or selling assets or shares there is usually a dilemma. In most cases, because of the preferred tax regime, vendors want to sell shares but, due to inherent liabilities, most acquirers want to purchase assets. This discussion may affect price and it may even prejudice a deal.

Tax issues aside, the sale of assets may work as follows. Assets may mean more than fixed or current assets. Often an acquirer will take on the liabilities of the company, such as creditors, bank debt and so forth, and also have to purchase intangible assets, such as goodwill, in order to complete the transaction.

These payments are made to the company – after all, they belong to the company – which means the only way you can gain access to these funds is to pay yourself a dividend or wind

---

up the business, clear any outstanding debt and take a final distribution from the residual proceeds. Obviously, timing is crucial because of those tax issues.

A share sale knows no such problems, since ownership of the company is passed to the acquirer, leaving the vendor to walk away into the sunset. Vendors may of course sell some rather than all their shares, which is sometimes known as a partial equity release. The sale could be to a trade buyer, a management candidate or an institutional acquirer. Some words of caution to the vendor, though. Although this releases value, hopefully in the form of cash, it inevitably means relinquishing control of the company to some degree.

Think carefully about the following points before considering this option.

- How will you realise the balance of your investment, and when?

- Are you happy with the covenants that will be placed on you in relation to:
  - how you operate;
  - how and what remuneration you will receive;
  - the strategic direction of the business; and
  - the management of the business?

- If in this exercise you end up as a minority shareholder (less than 51 per cent) you can be out voted – no fun if you have been used to being in charge.

On the upside, though, depending on the deal you strike, you may potentially be able to realise significant value, sometimes more than a pro rata value of the whole, and have the opportunity to participate in the company's future.

CHAPTER **12**

Finding the Right Buyer

ONCE YOU HAVE DETERMINED to sell, for whatever reason, the most important step is finding your dream acquirer. A summary of potential acquirers can be found in later in the book but, along with these categories, be clear as to whom you will not sell your business. I have just completed a transaction where the list of whom not to sell to was longer than the list of possible purchasers.

As always it's a question of saying you don't know what you don't know! In other words, there could be organisations out there desperate to acquire that don't know you are for sale. It's important then to make the best use of your resources. In other words, 'max out' the contacts and knowledge of your advisers and keep up to date with your industry sector.

There are lots of 'buy-build' corporates out there. Identify gaps in the market that your business could fill. Think about complementary products and services or even geographical gaps. It goes without saying that you should always consider global markets. It is possible that, provided you have groomed and positioned your business correctly, buyers will find you.

These are some of the areas you need to verify before you go too far down the road with an acquirer. Here are some questions to ask yourself.

Have they got the funding or access to funding?

This does not necessarily mean they have got a shed load of cash in their balance sheet (although that may be very attractive), but it does mean that they have access to funds from an appropriate source.

Although it is true that many transactions are funded using the vendor's own funds or his company's, an acquirer wholly reliant on this source of cash is possibly less attractive.

Will their culture fit with yours?

If you intend to cut and run you may not necessarily care, but my experience says you probably will, particularly if you are a founder owner-manager. The question becomes important if you have to work with new owners for any period of time.

Checking out the culture of an acquirer is a difficult process, though you will gain a greater sense of it throughout negotiations, especially if you are selling to a business of a similar ownership structure to yourself. Of course, you may at this stage have gone so far down the disposal negotiations that the lure of the pot of cash is too much to resist, even though you have realised that the ideological fit is less than ideal.

This is a difficult call. In one deal I recently completed, the acquirers were coy at the start of the negotiations. But as time progressed, it became clear that one of the vendors, who had decided to roll some of his consideration into the new venture, was likely to experience problems with the incoming management team. In this case we were able to change the structure of the deal almost at the last minute, allowing the vendor to take all his sale proceeds at completion and shorten his ongoing commitment to the company. However, we had to tread very carefully round this and it certainly could have been a deal breaker.

One way of gaining some sort of insight into the new owners is a 'mystery shopping trip'. This will at least demonstrate to you their attitude to customer relationships. Also establish as soon as possible how they interact with staff, their view of training and development and so forth. These issues give you a good feel for cultural beliefs.

How fit are the management team?

Vendors need to know the aptitude of the incoming management team, both in terms of their skill set and the depth and width of their knowledge. In other words, what can they bring to the party? This is vital if you are reliant on them to generate sufficient profits to allow the redemption of your loan notes. Ask who will be involved and at what level.

Are there synergistic products and services?

Where the acquirer is a corporate as opposed to an MBI candidate or the transaction is an MBO, does the acquirer's business have products and services that will not only sit happily with yours, but will enhance your position? Again, this is fairly crucial when you have a deal based on increasing performance related to an earn-out, for example. (This is an arrangement by which sellers of a business receive additional future payment, usually based on future earnings.)

Are the proper exit routes in place?

If you have carried out a partial equity release, you should be comfortable with the acquirer's own exit plans. Do they sit well with your own options? They could include refinancing but can also include floatation or a sale to a trade buyer. Establish what, who and when, and make sure you are entirely happy with the longer-term plans.

CONFIDENTIALITY – WHY IT'S IMPORTANT TO THE VENDOR

Confidentiality is important for both sides in the transaction. For the vendor's point of view a breach can wreak havoc with their existing business. At some point in the proceedings it becomes necessary to distribute valuable information to quite a number of interested parties, but timing it everything.

Customers

It is unlikely that it will be appropriate to notify your customers of an intention to sell. On the other hand, where your business performance is dependent on critical customers, your acquirer is going to want assurance of their continued support possibly prior to completing the deal.

I have been involved in several deals where the acquirer is adamant they must have 'face' time with key customers before finally committing to the transaction. This can be very worrying for a vendor, concerned that such meetings will unsettle a relationship and possibly result in its irretrievable loss while the deal may not come to fruition.

Where contracts with key customers are in place that are legally transferable on a sale, it is often possible to negotiate around face-to-face meetings. If not, this is a matter that should be left until the last moment, with NDAs being secured from both the customer and the acquirer.

Suppliers

As with customers, these are sensitive arrangements and particularly important where credit payments are involved. Assurances that a possible sale does not imply any financial difficulties for the supplier are important. Once again, if you have solus supplier arrangements, novation of contracts is vital.

▶

Funders

Obviously dependent on the type of funder. Incumbent equity investors will have a keen interest in the transaction. Indeed, they may even be able to prevent it. Debt funders, in other words bankers, will have to be fully repaid, even on a share transfer, before a deal is completed.

While it is not necessary to inform your bank until a deal has been agreed in principle, an outline discussion on the overall plan is probably not a bad idea at an earlier stage, particularly if your relationship is sound.

Competitors

Oh, how the competition loves to hear that a business is for sale! As soon as they have any inkling, your rivals will use this knowledge to lever a stronger market position. So, unless you can spot a distinct advantage in letting it be known you are up for sale, robust denial is essential.

Rumours spread swiftly, and if you hear one about your business on the grapevine try to establish how the news was leaked. Always take action against the perpetrator, especially if it has come from a source where an NDA has been signed.

Employees and management

Subject to the size of your business and particularly the number of staff you employ, under the Information Consultation Directive you may be legally bound to consult with your staff/representatives.

From March 2008 any company with 50 or more staff will be required to do this in advance of taking the decision to sell.

But, legal requirements aside, the quality and commitment of your workforce is value related in most cases. It could there- fore be absolutely essential that key staff be informed before and sometimes well before completion.

As ongoing job security and personal development are

▶

paramount in many cases, if it becomes essential for a meeting to take place between staff and acquirer before a deal is struck, you need to manage this process at a micro level.

From a confidentiality point of view, you certainly need to elicit written agreements from the potential acquirer that there will be no poaching of staff should the deal not go ahead. You may also wish to consider some sort of incentive to keep your staff motivated and committed to the new company if the deal goes ahead. This could include share options or bonus schemes, for example.

Your staff and management

Employee rights are protected under TUPE and this includes sale of shares and sale of assets. It also provides protection for staff attached to contracts that provide goods or services, should that contract be transferred to a third party.

As previously mentioned, you may have a legal obligation to communicate with staff representatives. Consultation requires you to engage in a two-way discussion. In other words, it's not a fait accompli: it requires you to consider and respond to employee representations. While there's no need to reach unanimous agreement with staff, any withdrawal of cooperation by the workforce will probably affect or even threaten your deal.

As part of your grooming process, you might consider the removal of excess staff via a redundancy programme. Take professional advice and always follow the correct procedures, since claims for unfair dismissal will blight a sale. Be sure that redundancies really will make the business a more attractive proposition.

CHAPTER 13

The Right Deal for You

THERE IS LITTLE POINT GOING through all the heartache of trying to sell your business or even completing the sale only to discover that actually it isn't quite the deal you desired. With this thought in mind, check out some of those critical issues to be aware of at the start, during and after the transaction completes.

Tax planning

It is only natural that one of your key requirements will be to minimise the tax you owe on any gain you receive when selling the business. When in 1998 the government introduced a scheme whereby vendors could reduce their capital-gains tax (CGT) to as little as 10 per cent for a high-rate taxpayer or 5 per cent for a basic-rate payer, the desire to ensure vendors complied with this process increased.

This tax relief (also known as taper relief) is available to individuals but not to companies. So if all the shares are owned by a company rather than an individual, it's not possible to claim this taper relief, although there may be other options available such as indexation allowances.

A critical point linked to this beneficial tax relief is that it works best when it applies to the sale of business assets in businesses where the shares have been owned for two or more years. Of course, nonbusiness assets can be sold but the relief is not as great at 24 per cent for a high-rate taxpayer and 12 per cent for a basic-rate payer.

A TIP

You may well be thinking that all the assets you hold in your business must be business assets, but, alas, that is not necessarily the case. Business assets can be defined as follows:

- assets that are used within the business (and since April 2004 this applies to partnerships and sole traders);

- shares in a qualifying company (this must be a trading company or the holding company of a trading group).

Although this may seem quite simple, a number of my clients have been surprised to discover that certain assets they assumed to be business assets have subsequently turned out not to be so. Examples included substantial cash sums residing in the balance sheet in excess of normal working capital required and income derived from subletting of premises when property rental was not part of the business's main operations – so beware!

In circumstances in which a sale includes what Revenue and Customs ultimately defines as including business and non-business assets, then proportional relief will be given.

Pre-Revenue and Customs approval of a structure is always advisable, because without this your potential sale proceeds could be diluted by an increase in the amount of tax you are expected to pay. These Revenue and Customs clearances are not something you should embark on alone. They are complex and need technical advice, so always consult a professional.

Of course you may, with proper planning, be able to eliminate all tax payments, but this requires you to dispose of your shares when you are a nonresident of the UK or when you are not ordinarily a resident of the UK. You must not live in the UK for five years in order to comply. Clearly, this presents all sorts of difficulties, not least concluding a sale when you are not even resident in the country.

One other way of eliminating an immediate capital gain is what is called a share-for-share exchange. In other words, instead of taking cash or loan notes as your consideration, you have shares in the acquiring company. This also applies if part of the consideration is taken in what are called qualifying corporate bonds (QCBs). Basically, this is a nonconvertible, nonredeemable sterling security issued on normal commercial terms. Any gain on that particular element of the consideration is deferred until the bond is redeemed or disposed of.

If you are anticipating your consideration in part on a deferred or contingent basis, beware the tax implications. It is likely that you will have to pay the capital gain on the sum even before you receive it, unless the deferred period extends to more than 18 months, in which case you may be able to pay the tax by instalments over a maximum of eight years.

If these payments are not made to you, in other words the acquirers can't pay, you may be able to claim back tax paid. And, where the consideration is contingent and estimations of payments were higher than those actually made, you will be able to claim back against tax paid in advance.

There are of course other planning devices available for the astute vendor.

Presale dividends

These are appropriate if the effective income-tax rate on the dividend is lower than the CGT rate. This works by reducing the value of the company and so the CGT payable.

However if you have a qualifying company selling business assets, this option is unlikely to be tax-effective except, for example, if you were wishing to realise the investment in your business by way of liquidating the company.

Compensation for loss of office

Up to £30,000 can effectively taken on a tax-free basis, although this may potentially reduce the value of the business. You need to establish that Revenue and Customs does not regard this as hidden consideration.

Pension pot top-ups

These are worth considering but need to be carried out well in advance of the sale or they could be potentially unsustainable in reducing tax liabilities.

General timing

If you sell your business at the start of a new tax year, you won't save tax per se, but you could hold onto the tax element of the fund for 12 months longer.

Transferring assets to your spouse

Do this either pre- or post-sale and not only could it alleviate CGT but may also wield a potential impact on inheritance tax and income-tax gains on the proceeds of sale that are invested.

If your plans include using the consideration to invest in another business, you may be able to obtain what is called business asset rollover relief. To receive this, your funds need to be invested in ordinary shares and there are various rules about the type of business and the length of the investment.

You may, subject to Revenue and Customs' approval, be able to gift business assets, and this includes shares (in unlisted companies), so tax will be paid only when the receiver of the gift disposes of it.

FULL TAX EXEMPTION

The following are some examples whereby CGT is either partially or fully exempt.

Transfer between husband and wife

You must be legally married and cohabiting. Transfer means to sell or give an asset. In these circumstances there is neither a chargeable gain nor an allowable loss.

Selling your main residence

Crucially, it must be your main house, not a second home, and the land must amount to less than half a hectare (about 1½ acres). In these circumstance you will not pay CGT. However, be careful if you have ever run a business from home, as this may affect this right.

Gifts to charity

If you are feeling particularly benevolent and you can give or sell the business for less than fair market value you will be relieved of CGT.

I am also sure you will be delighted to hear that any sums you receive in relation to the following do not attract tax payments of any sort:

- personal-injury claims;

- life-insurance payout (where you are the original benefactor);

- proceeds from gambling;

- compensation payments for missold pensions.

Whom to tell in Revenue and Customs

There are certain statutory procedures that you will be required to comply with as part of your sale. Your lawyer will probably deal with this but she needs to notify Revenue and Customs and fill in any appropriate forms for Companies House notification.

Warranties and indemnities

The sale process in an ideal world should leave you with not only as much cash as possible but confident that you have no liabilities for the business you have sold.

Of course, our acquirer wants to minimise risk, so a halfway position must be struck to facilitate the deal. This process is managed by the utilisation of warranties and indemnities. These are a standard part of the final contract.

A warranty is a representation made by you, the vendor, and will constitute a statement of fact about the state of the business such as, 'There is no outstanding litigation.' If you make a statement of this nature that subsequently turns out to be untrue, the acquirer can bring an action for damages under a breach of contract clause.

An indemnity is a graver concern, for, as vendor, you are actually promising to make a payment should certain circumstances occur, negating the need for a claim for breach of contract. For example, an indemnity could commit you to making a payment if back tax bills relating to a time when the company was under your control are issued by Revenue and Customs.

And warranties and indemnities are not solely linked to tax and litigation matters. It is just as likely that you will be requested to provide one or other of these types of assurances, including:

- health-and-safety aspects of your business and its premises;

- ownership of intellectual property and patents or environmental matters.

In order to manage the risk you will be exposed to you should always:

- agree time limits on claims – two years is usual for most, with seven for tax warranties;

- have a maximum claim level (I recommend that this be never more than the total consideration you receive);

- have a minimum level for claims (you don't want acquirers making claims for a couple of hundred pounds, for instance);

- make sure the procedure for making a claim is clearly documented and understood – for example, number of days, post, email, acknowledgement issues.

Also, be advised you may well have to lodge some sums in an escrow account (a holding account) against some of your indemnities provided, which effectively ties up your cash for an agreed period.

If your acquirer is an MBO team you will definitely be able to reduce the extent of these representations, as the management will have been running the company and should know as much about the business as you do.

If you currently own the business with an institutional investor he is very unlikely to have any involvement at all in the provision of warranties and indemnities and this is, in my experience, a nonnegotiable fact.

My practical experience of claims is that an acquirer will resort to this only as a last option, particularly when no escrow account exists and where legal action is necessary to prove damages. However, hundreds of claims are made, so don't be complacent.

Finally, don't forget that you can limit claim potential by ensuring you make a good and thorough disclosure of all issues you are aware of that could lead to a claim. Your legal advisers will strengthen your position the best they can. And don't forget also that it is possible to insure against claims. There are numerous providers on the Web. It's an extra cost, of course, but it may bring you peace of mind.

Anti-embarrassment clauses

Vendors always fear they could have got more for a business if only they had held on a bit longer. Worse still is the prospect that the new owner has carved out a crafty deal to sell on the company swiftly at some highly inflated price to make a killing.

Although it is not always the case, an astute vendor can provide for some sort of insurance against these potential lost revenues by way of an anti-embarrassment clause in the sale-and-purchase agreement. The writing of this clause is potentially complex and it would be your legal team's responsibility to ensure it is viable and enforceable.

Usually, such a clause is limited in time and there's often a declining scale of percentages relating to compensatory payments. For example, an agreement is likely to permit a greater payment if the new owners dispose of the business within a year than within three years.

This clause is all about taking a reasonable position. Ensure it covers a time period from when heads of terms are agreed – in other words, if your period of potential participation is three years' time and will not have elapsed if a potential sale is started in Month 35 and doesn't complete until Month 42!

How will funds reach you?

If you have read earlier advice on raising finance, you will appreciate the many sources of funding available to the acquirer. However, that doesn't necessarily mean you the vendor will receive all the money for the business in a single tranche. In fact, this is increasingly uncommon.

Vendor loans and deferred-contingent consideration are just two of the ways in which you are likely to be assisting in the acquisition funding. You may even take some shares in the new venture or continue to work for the company as either an employee or consultant.

Clearly, where any sums are not advanced immediately on completion, you will want as much certainty as possible that you will eventually receive them, but ultimately you will have to take a commercial view on the risk.

YOUR FEES

Whatever the deal structure, you will have your professional fees to pay. Usually these are taken out of the initial consideration you secure, not out of deferred sums.

So what you get in a share sale is likely to have the following deductions from it:

- initial consideration

less:

- your legal fees;

- your corporate financier's fee;

- broker's fees (if relevant);

- tax advice;

- IFA advice;

- VAT on these as relevant …

… and at a later stage your CGT.

The timing of your sale is important in relation to the last of these, since this tax is payable in the January (the 31st) after the end of the fiscal year in which you complete your deal.

For example the tax payable on a deal completed on 4 April 2006 (the day before the end of the fiscal year) is due on 31

January 2007. However, if it is completed on 6 April (the day after the fiscal year ends), the CGT doesn't become payable until 31 January 2008. (By the way, if you complete on 5 April that means the tax is payable in 2007.)

Don't forget that you may have to live off those sale funds for some time. That of course may be the plan, but you may actually be prevented from working (at least in the industry sector you have sold) for a period of time.

This restriction (or restrictive covenant) is meant to prevent you from competing with the new owners and can, in certain circumstances, be for long periods.

Stay in or get out?

My motto for vendors is clear: sell out, get out and take your consideration in cash. Spend some of your newfound spare time counting the cash. A client who sold her business for £15 million telephoned her bank the day after the deal completed. 'I promise not to do this again,' she said. 'But just how much interest did I earn last night while I was asleep?'

For all the reasons mentioned so far, this is generally the least painful. However, you may not always have this option. Assuming you don't, here are some of the issues you need to consider.

- Will you stay as an employee or as a director? Chances are it will be the latter, so get yourself a good directors' service contract, take legal advice on its compilation but ensure it covers:
  - notice periods (on both sides);
  - expenses policy;
  - job requirements, duties, hours;
  - golden goodbyes;
  - incentives and bonus agreements;
  - holiday and leave agreements;
  - restrictive covenants and restraints of trade agreements.

- Be advised that by law these contracts have to be open for inspection by the shareholders.

- Ensure you are happy with the directors' and officers' liability insurance and that it contains 'run-off cover' for after you leave office. In other words, it covers directors who are no longer in post. This should be for a minimum of three years post-departure.

- For those vendors on earn-outs you should have structured this so it is transparent but you certainly need to ensure you:
  - are party to any discussions that could affect its value and that you have a right of veto on such decisions;
  - have right of access to all information needed to verify it.

- You should have access to all strategic documents that concern the future direction of the business. If you are a director you should of course be party to their creation but if you are just an employee you may not.

- Consider the implications of your backing out of the ongoing role in the business sooner than planned due either to:
  - ill health;
  - disagreements; or even
  - death.

The effect on earn-outs is pretty important. You need to pre-agree this as part of the completion arrangements.

A final checklist for the seller

- Ensure that your plans for after the transaction completes – regarding those aspects of your personal life – are realistic and well thought through.

- Check the value of security offered for any consideration that is deferred.

- If you are of an altruistic nature, be happy in the quality of the opportunities for the staff you leave behind. They are protected to an extent under TUPE, but that does not prevent them from being made redundant or being offered other opportunities.

- If you are attached to the brand name you are selling, you may wish to have covenants in place to ensure it is not used in a manner you are unhappy with.

- Are all your statutory books and records up to date, including the whereabouts of the share certificate?

APPENDIX 1

Glossary

Acquisition: Any deal whereby the bidder ends up with 50 per cent or more of the target is called an acquisition. A bidder is the entity that makes the purchase or the offer to purchase. The target is the entity being purchased, or the entity in which a stake is being purchased. The vendor is the entity that sells or disposes of the target entity.

BIMBO: A combination of management buy-out and buy-in whereby the team buying the business includes both existing management and new managers.

Bond: The generic name for a tradable loan security issued by governments and companies as a means of raising capital. Government bonds are known as gilts or Treasury stock.

Capital holiday: The ability to take a period of time on a loan-repayment programme when only interest is paid on the loan rather than interest and capital.

CCJ: County Court judgment – a judgment issued by the County Court that encompasses a requirement on the individual to clear a debt.

Contingent: A liability that, dependent on certain conditions or occurrences, may arise.

Current asset: Something owed to or owned by a business, such as proceeds from a sale that is payable within the next 12 months.

Data room: A room of confidential information related to a disposal or acquisition, controlled by the company's advisers.

Debenture: A legal document that formalises the lender's charge over the assets of the company.

Debt: This may include bank loans, overdrafts and lease financing and may be long or short term, secured or unsecured. The lender receives interest at an agreed rate and in the event that this is not paid may be entitled to take control of and sell certain assets owned by the company. A lender does not, however, generally have a share in the ownership of the business.

Development capital: Also known as expansion capital, this may be venture-capital financing used for expansion of an already established company.

Discrete: An adjective describing a separate entity or part.

Drag-along clause: A clause conferring the right of majority shareholders to force minority shares to sell their shares when the majority dispose of theirs.

Due diligence: One of the main processes that takes place before a transaction (such as a MBO or MBI) is completed. The aim is to ensure that there is nothing that contradicts the financier's understanding of the current state and potential of the business. The individual elements of due diligence may include commercial due diligence (markets, product and customers), a market report (marketing study), an accountant's report (trading record, net asset and taxation position) and legal due diligence (implications of litigation, entitlement to assets and intellectual property issues).

EBIT: Earnings before interest and tax.

EBITDA: Earnings before interest, tax, depreciation and amortisation. EBITDA is a measure of cash flow. By the exclusion of interest, taxes, depreciation and amortisation, the amount of money a company is bringing in can be clearly seen.

EMI scheme: Employee management incentive scheme – a share purchase scheme which allows employees to purchase shares via a salary sacrifice or bonus programme.

Equity: The term used to describe shares in a business conveying ownership of that business. The shareholders may be entitled to dividends. If a business fails, the shareholders will receive only a distribution on winding up after the lenders and creditors have been paid. An equity investment, therefore, has a higher risk attached to it than that facing a bank lender and thus the return that the shareholders demand on their money is typically higher. The most common source of equity finance for buy-outs is the venture capital market.

Escrow account: A bank account into which funds are retained and managed by advisers (usually solicitors) relating to a transaction to allow payment to be made if warranties or indemnities are breached.

Exit (realisation): The point at which the institutional investors realise their investment. Venture capitalists may, depending on the business and their own situation, look to achieve an exit in anything from a few months to 10 years. Exits generally occur via trade sales, secondary management buy-outs and flotation on the stock market or by write-off if the investment ends in receivership.

Goodwill: The difference between the price that is paid for a business and the value of its assets.

High-yield (junk) bonds: Bonds that offer high rates of interest but with correspondingly higher risk attached to the capital.

IBO: An institutional buy-out. This is when a private equity house acquires a business directly from the vendor. Often the target's management will take a small stake.

IPO: Initial public offer. Shares in a company have been placed on a stock exchange. An IPO is always just the first time a company's shares are listed – if a company has a listing on another market or in another country, then the listing is not an IPO, merely a secondary, or additional, listing.

IRR: Internal rate of return. The average annual compound rate of return received by an investor over the life of their investment. This is a key indicator used by institutions in appraising their investments.

Joint venture: A venture formed by two or more companies.

Keyman cover: Insurance cover payable on the death of a critical individual in a business, allowing the company to replace the dead person's skills.

LBO: Leveraged buy-out, an American term. The takeover of a company by investors who use the company's own assets as collateral to raise the money that finances the bid. Normally, the loans are then repaid either from the company's cash flow, or by selling some of its assets.

LBU: Leveraged build-up. A venture-capital firm builds up the company it owns by acquiring smaller companies to amalgamate into the larger firm, thus increasing the total value of its investments through synergies between the acquired companies.

Loan note: A form of vendor finance or deferred payment. The purchaser acts as a borrower, agreeing to make payments to the holder of the transferable loan note at a specified future date.

MBI: Management buy-in. The company is sold to a combination of a new team of managers, with the new management team taking a majority stake. This often happens with family firms who have no one to pass the company on to, so they sell it to a management team. The old owners sometimes retain a small stake. The management team often includes a venture-capital firm; however, if that firm takes a majority stake, then the deal is classed as an IBO rather than an MBI.

MBO: Management buy-out. This is the purchase of a business by its management, usually in cooperation with outside financiers. Buyouts vary in size, scope and complexity but the key feature is that the managers acquire an equity interest in their business, sometimes a controlling stake, for a relatively modest personal investment. The existing owners sell most or usually all of their investment to the managers and their co-investors. If the outside financier (the venture-capital firm, for instance) takes a majority stake, then the deal is not an MBO but an IBO.

Merger: A true merger is actually quite rare. Many acquisitions are described as mergers but, in a true merger, there is a one-for-one share swap, for shares in the new company. If the swap is not on equal terms, then it is an acquisition.

Mezzanine finance: This is often used to bridge the gap between the secured debt a business can support, the available equity and the purchase price. Because of this, and because it normally ranks behind senior debt in priority of repayment, unsecured mezzanine debt commands a significantly higher rate of return than senior debt and often carries warrants (options to buy ordinary shares) to subscribe for ordinary shares. It ranks behind more formal borrowing contracts and is thus referred to as subordinated or intermediate debt.

MIS: Management information system – either a manual or computerised programme that gives the users access to a suite of critical data about the performance of the company.

Net asset value: This is the value of the company based on the valuation of the assets less any liabilities that it has in its balance sheet.

Newco: A new company formed to affect the buy-out by acquiring the operating subsidiaries.

Novation rights: The right to transfer ownership of an asset, lease or contract to a new party.

Ordinary shares: Ordinary shareholders carry full rights to participate in the business through voting in general meetings. They are entitled to payment of a dividend out of profits and ultimately repayment of capital in the event of liquidation, but only after other claims have been met. As owners of the company, the ordinary shareholders bear the greatest risk, but also enjoy the fruits of corporate success in the form of higher dividends and/or capital gains.

PBIT: Profit before interest and tax.

PE ratio: The price–earnings ratio is one of the most commonly used measures of value in financial circles. It expresses the value in terms of a multiple of profits. For any company quoted on the Stock Exchange, this figure can be easily calculated and is published daily in the *Financial Times*.

Phantom share scheme: An agreement between a company that certain members of the management team have an assumed right to participate in the proceeds of the sale of the business without actually owning physical shares.

Pre-emption rights: The requirement of an incumbent shareholder to offer those shares to other specified parties or corporates on certain criteria before offering them to third parties.

Preference shares: These fall between debt and equity. They usually carry no voting rights and have preferential rights over ordinary shareholders regarding dividends and ultimate repayment of capital in the event of liquidation.

Private equity: This is an increasingly widely used term in Europe and is generally interchangeable with venture capital, but some commentators use it to refer only to the management buy-out and buy-in investment sector.

Privatisation: A government, council or other state-owned entity disposes of a company or stake in a company that it owns. The company, or part of the company, moves from public to private ownership.

Public buy-in: Individual or group of individuals purchasing a majority stake in a publicly quoted company.

Public-to-private buy-out: This involves the management or a private equity provider making an offer for the shares of a publicly quoted company, then taking the company private.

Ratchet: A mechanism whereby management's equity stake may be increased (or decreased) on the occurrence of various future events, typically when the institutional investor's returns exceed a particular target rate.

Reverse takeover: An unlisted company acquires a smaller, listed, company, thus achieving a stock-market listing 'through the back door'. The acquisition is carried out by the listed company's issuing new shares in order to acquire the unlisted company. As the unlisted company is larger than the listed one, the bidder has to issue so many new shares that the owners of the unlisted company end up with a controlling stake in the listed company.

Secondary buy-out: The management team, in conjunction with a private equity funder, acquire the business, allowing the existing private equity supplier to exit from its investment.

Second-round financing: Most companies need more than the initial injection of capital, whether to enable them to expand into new markets, develop more production capacity or overcome temporary problems. There can be several rounds of financing.

Senior debt: Debt provided by a bank, usually secured and ranking ahead of other loans and borrowings in the event of a winding-up.

Sensitivity analysis: The process used by funders and corporates to analyse information using what-if scenarios.

Shares: Certificates or book entries representing ownership in a business.

SME: Small to medium-sized enterprise – usually a business with fewer than 250 staff.

Solus relationship: A single relationship that precludes utilisation of others for the supply, distribution or sale of goods or services.

Startup capital: Capital used to establish a company from scratch or within the first few months of its existence. Risky, but with huge potential returns for the very successful.

Subordinated loans: Loans that rank after other debt. These loans will normally be repayable after other debt has been serviced and are thus more risky from the lender's point of view. Mezzanine finance is an example of a subordinated loan.

Syndicated investment: Where an investment is too large, complex or risky, the lead investor may seek other financiers to share the investment. This process is known as syndication.

Synergy: The phenomenon whereby the whole is greater than the sum of its individual parts. In business terms, the combined effort would be more effective than the sum of the separate efforts of the component parts.

Tag-along clause: The right of shareholders to sell their shares at the same time as other shareholders and at the same value.

Trade sale: A common method of exit, this is a sale to a trade buyer. This can either allow management to withdraw from the business, or open up the prospect of working in a larger enterprise.

Vendor finance: Can be in the form of either deferred loans from, or shares subscribed by, the vendor. The vendor may well take shares alongside the management in the new entity. This category of finance is generally used when the vendor's expectation of the value of the business is higher than that of management and the institutions backing them.

Venture capital: Equity finance in an unquoted, and usually quite young, company to enable it to start up, expand or restructure its operations entirely. It's cheaper than bank finance initially because paying dividends can be deferred; it also provides a strategic partner – but it implies handing over some control, a share of earnings and decisions over future sales.

Warranties and indemnities: Legal confirmation given by the seller, regarding matters such as tax or contingent liabilities, to assure the buyer that any undisclosed liabilities that subsequently come to light will be settled by the seller.

Resources

Resource organisation websites

UK Stock Exchanges, London Stock Exchange, UKLA Official List (Main Market)

In mid-2004, about 2,400 companies were quoted on the Main Market of the London Stock Exchange known as the UKLA Official List.

Joining is a two-stage process: to the Official List by the UK Listing Authority (now part of the FSA); and also to trading by the Exchange.

http://www.fsa.gov.uk/officiallist/

AIM

AIM opened in 1995 and is run by the London Stock Exchange. In mid-2004, about 1,050 companies were members of AIM. Entry criteria are less onerous than for the Main Market. Once a company has been on AIM for two years it can, if it chooses, request admittance to the Main Market.

http://www.londonstockexchange.com

OFEX

Launched in October 1995, it currently lists around 160 companies. This is not a regulated market but OFEX member firms must comply with the London Stock Exchange rulebook.

http://www.ofex.com

ShareMark

Founded in June 2000 as an Internet-based facility for trading shares through regular auctions. Run by the Aylesbury-based stockbroker the Share Centre and its parent company, Share PLC.

http://www.sharemark.co.uk

Useful organisations

Academy for Chief Executives (ACE)
The Nexus Building
Letchworth Garden City
Hertfordshire SG6 3TA
0800 0370 250

http://www.chiefexecutive.com

ACE provides a confidential learning environment for noncompeting chief executives and managing directors from all sectors of industry, commerce and the nonprofit sector.

ACAS
Brandon House
180 Borough High Street
London SE1 1LW
020 7210 3613

http://www.acas.org.uk

ACAS aims to improve organisations and working life through better employment relations. It provides up-to-date information, independent advice and high-quality training, and works with employers and employees to solve problems and improve performance.

ACAS has a number of regional offices. You must make an appointment before visiting.

Association of Chartered Certified Accountants
64 Finnieston Square
Glasgow G3 8DT
0141 582 2000

http://www.accaglobal.com

The Association of Chartered Certified Accountants is the largest international accountancy body in the world. Its mission is to provide professional opportunities and access for people of ability around the world, to achieve and promote the highest professional, ethical and governance standards, to advance public interest and to be the global leader in the profession.

Companies House
Crown Way
Maindy
Cardiff CF14 3UZ
0870 3333 636

http://www.companieshouse.gov.uk/

The main functions of Companies House include incorporating and dissolving limited companies, examining and storing company information and making all this information available to the public. The site also gives a lot of useful information with regards to running a company.

Dun & Bradstreet
D&B United Kingdom Customer Service Department
Westminster House
Portland Street
Manchester M1 3HU
0870 2432 344

http://www.dnb.com

Dun & Bradstreet is a provider of global business information, tools and insight, enabling customers to make critical business decisions.

Experian
UK headquarters: Talbot House
Talbot Street
Nottingham N80 1TH
0115 941 0888

http://www.experian.com

Experian helps organisations find the best prospects and make informal decisions to personalise and develop customer relationships.

It supports the direct marketing, business information, decision support and outsourcing requirements of more than 40,000 organisations.

Institute of Directors (IoD)
116 Pall Mall
London SW1Y 5ED
020 7839 1233

http://www.iod.com

With a worldwide membership, the IoD provides a professional network that reaches into every corner of the business community. Membership spans a whole spectrum of business leadership, from the largest public companies to the smallest private firms. Members receive benefits including advice, training, conferences and publications. The IoD represents its members' concerns to the government and provides professional business support wherever needed.

Law Society
Main London office: Law Society's Hall
113 Chancery Lane
London WC2A 1PL
020 7242 1222

http://www.lawsociety.org.uk

The Law Society is the regulatory and representative body for 116,000 solicitors in England and Wales, with public responsibilities including regulating and representing solicitors, supporting solicitors and influencing law reform.

The society has a number of offices; check their website for the one nearest you.

Vistage International (Previously TEC International)
UK office: One Crown Walk
Jewry Street
Winchester
Hampshire SO23 8BD
01962 841 188

http://www.vistage.com

Vistage International helps companies outperform the competition. Business leaders come to Vistage to accelerate the growth of their business and of themselves. Growth comes from one-to-one executive coaching, access to a group of trusted peers and entry into the worldwide network of more than 10,000 executives.

UK Patent Office
Concept House
Cardiff Road
Newport
South Wales NP10 8QQ
0845 9500 505

http://www.patent.gov.uk

The UK Patent Office helps stimulate innovation and enhance the international competitiveness of British industry and commerce. It offers customers an accessible, high-quality, value-for-money system for granting intellectual property rights such as copyright, designs, patents and trademarks.

Websites for general information

http://www.cbi.org.uk
http://www.dti.gov.uk
http://www.dti.gov.uk/cld/condocs/htm
http://www.icsa.org.uk
http://www.independentdirector.co.uk
http://www.iod.com/factsheets
http://www.ukonline.gov.uk

Websites for businesses for sale

http://www.biztrader.com
http://www.business-engineering.co.uk (manufacturers and contractors)
http://www.businessesforsale.co.uk
http://www.business-exchange-plc.co.uk
http://www.businessforsale.com
http://www.businesssale.co.uk

http://www.business-sale.com
http://www.byabiz.com
http://www.carpediemcorporate.co.uk
http://www.companiesforsale.uk.com
http://www.companysales.net
http://www.DaltonsBusiness.com
http://www.diverco.co.uk
http://www.forumcommercial.com
http://www.loot.com
http://www.matrixmergers.co.uk
http://www.redwoods.co.uk
http://www.startinbusiness.co.uk
http://www.turnerandco.com
http://www.ukbusinessbase.com

British Franchise Association
Established in 1977, the BFA acts in the interests of the industry as a whole in assessing and accrediting franchising companies which meet its criteria for the structure of the business etc.

http://www.thebfa.org

British Venture Capital Association
The BVCA represents more than 170 UK-based private equity and venture-capital firms, the vast majority of all such firms in the UK. It is the public face of the industry, providing services to its members, investors and entrepreneurs as well as the government and media.

http://www.bvca.co.uk

IMPORTANT NOTE

All the legal documents contained in the following appendices (appendices 3–9) are meant as a guide only. Independent legal advice should always be taken.

Letter of Intent

[Date]

Ms J Haigh
Corporate Finance
[Address]

SUBJECT TO CONTRACT and without Prejudice

Dear Ms Haigh

Project [name]

Further to receiving the Information Memorandum in respect of Project [name] we would like to introduce ourselves.

We are a local company founded in [year] and together with our two sister companies we turnover in excess of [£turnover] per annum employing [number] office-based staff and pay rolling [number] temporary workers per week.

We feel Project [name] is a company that may be able to add value and complement our existing businesses, and are keen to move on to further discussions with the vendors. We have built our reputation within niche markets both locally and nationally by providing a first-class service based on our core values of honesty and integrity. We have excellent staff retention, investing heavily in training and staff-development programmes.

Please find below details as requested:

1. Our indicative offer for the purchase of Project [name] is [£amount].

2. The above is based on the information provided to us.

3. In respect of due diligence, we anticipate the following requirements:

    *   meeting the vendors to obtain a full understanding of the business and how it operates;

    *   an examination of contracts with customers;

    *   further information in connection with the annual accounts from the auditors;

    *   examination of all employment contracts and meetings and discussions with [employee names].

4. The purchase will be financed by our own funds and our own bankers, with whom we have already had discussions.

We trust the above is of interest to you and look forward to progressing things further. However, should you require any further information or clarification of any of the above points, please do not hesitate to contact me.

Yours sincerely
For [company]

_____

[Signature]

_____

[Name]

Heads of Terms

[Company]

Sales of entire issued share capital

Heads of Terms

1. **Parties to the Transaction**

Vendors:	[name]
Purchasers:	[name]
The Company:	[name]

2. **The Transaction**

   Subject to contract, the Vendors have agreed to sell and the Purchasers have agreed to buy, the entire issued share capital of [company] ('the Company') for a total consideration of [£amount], which includes:

   [£amount], in cash, on completion;

   a non-interest-bearing subordinated loan note with a value of [£amount], which will be issued, with payments to be made on each anniversary of completion, as follows:

Year 1	[£amount]
Year 2	[£amount]
Year 3	[£amount]
Year 4	[£amount]
Year 5	[£amount]

(this will be secured by a second charge over the assets of the business);

the [car], and [car] and private registrations, which will be transferred to the vendors on completion, at a value of [£ amount].

In addition, should the turnover of the business be greater than or equal to [£ amount] per annum, then a further payment of [£ amount] per annum in Years 2 to 5 will be made.

A new company will be formed by the Purchasers to effect this acquisition.

The outline terms agreed are set out in these Heads of Terms.

3. The Vendors will continue to run the Company in accordance with existing policies, trading terms, procedures and systems.

4. No other assets will be removed from the business between now and completion other than in the normal course of trade.

5. The full amount of [name]'s loan account will be repaid to the company prior to or at completion.

6. Any capital expenditure or material revenue expenditure incurred that might result in a commitment for the Purchasers post-completion will be notified as soon as reasonably possible to the Purchasers.

7. In the sale-and-purchase agreement, the Vendors will give such normal warranties and indemnities to the Company and in such form and scope as those normally provided by vendors.

8. [Name] will remain on the Board of Directors until the final payment of deferred consideration is paid. Terms under which [name] is to be remunerated are to be mutually agreed.

9. Prior to completion of the Transaction, the Vendors and Purchasers agree to negotiate leases on property held between the company and the Vendors' Directors' pension scheme.

10. The Vendors will agree to enter into restrictive covenants with the Purchasers in such form as those normally provided.

11. Prior to completion, the Purchasers and their advisers may need to undertake due-diligence investigations and the Vendors agree to allow them and their advisers full access to the Company, its senior personnel and accounting records, and to provide all such information as may be reasonably requested.

12. The parties intend to complete the transaction by [date].

13. Each party shall bear its own costs in relation to the negotiations leading up to legal completion of the Transaction contemplated in these Heads of Terms and for the preparation, signing and carrying into effect of the share sale-and-purchase agreement and of all ancillary documents/minutes etc. The Purchasers' solicitor shall draw up the sale-and-purchase agreement.

14. **Confidentiality**
The parties shall keep all aspects of this transaction confidential and shall not disclose details except to relevant professional advisers and to others who need to know of the transaction as part of the negotiation of the transaction, due-diligence and funding arrangements.

15. **Exclusivity**
In signing these Heads of Terms the Vendors agree to grant to the Purchasers a period of exclusivity up to [date], during which the Vendors agree not to sell or agree to sell or offer for sale, or enter into a commitment or negotiations to sell, their shareholdings, any part of their shareholdings or the trade and assets of the Company to any party other than the Purchasers.

16. **Announcements**
No announcement regarding the proposals in the Heads of Terms will be made other than in terms approved by the Vendors and Purchasers. All discussions and negotiations and the giving or receiving of information and documents shall be bound by confidentiality.

17. Binding Clauses

This clause and Clauses 14, 15, 16 and 18 of these Heads of Terms shall be binding on the parties mentioned herein upon the signing of these Heads of Terms. All other clauses are subject to contract and to the preparation and negotiation of formal legal documentation.

18. Governing Law

These Heads of Terms shall be governed by and construed in accordance with English law and all parties to these Heads of Terms hereby agree to submit for all purposes in connection with the Transaction to the exclusive jurisdiction of the English Courts.

19. HMRC Clearances

The transaction is conditional on the vendors securing the relevant clearances from HMRC in respect of the exchange in their shares for the loan notes.

The above fairly represents the matters agreed in respect of the proposed sale by the Vendors to the Purchasers of the entire issued share capital of [company].

_____

_____

[name]

For and on behalf of the Vendors   Date

_____

_____

[name]

For an on behalf of the Purchasers   Date

APPENDIX 5

Nondisclosure Agreement

Strictly Private & Confidential – Addressee Only

Corporate Finance	Your ref:
[address]	Our ref:
	Please reply to:

[Date]

Dear Sirs

[Name of Company] ('the Company')

We wish to investigate the business of the Company in connection with a proposed acquisition (the Permitted Purpose) and we will need access to certain information relating to the Company (the Confidential Information). For the purpose of this letter the Company and its directors, employees and advisers are referred to as 'the Disclosees'.

1. In consideration of your agreeing to supply, and so supplying, the Confidential Information to us and agreeing to enter into discussions with us, we hereby undertake and agree as follows:

    (a) To hold the Confidential Information in confidence and not to disclose or permit it to be made available to any person, firm or company (except to other Disclosees), without your prior consent.

(b) To use the Confidential Information only for the Permitted Purpose.

(c) To ensure that each person to whom disclosure of Confidential Information is made by us is fully aware in advance of our obligation under this letter and that, in the case of other potential providers of finance, each such person gives an undertaking in respect of the Confidential Information under the terms of this letter.

(d) Upon written demand from you, either to return the Confidential Information and any copies of it or to confirm to you in writing that, save as required by law or regulation, it has been destroyed. We shall not be required to return reports, notes or other material prepared by us or other Disclosees or on our or their behalf which incorporates Confidential Information (Secondary Information), provided that the Secondary Information is kept confidential.

(e) To keep confidential and not reveal to any person, firm or company (other than Disclosees) the fact of our investigation into the Company or that discussions or negotiations are taking place or have taken place between us in connection with the proposed transaction or that potential investors/acquirers are being sought for the Company.

(f) That no one give any warranty or make any representation as to the accuracy or otherwise of the Confidential Information, save as may subsequently be agreed.

2. Nothing in paragraphs 1(a) to (f) of this letter shall apply to any information or Confidential Information:

    (a) Which at the time of its disclosure is in the public domain.

    (b) Which after disclosure comes into the public domain for any reason except our failure, or failure on the part of any Disclosee, to comply with the terms of this letter.

    (c) Which is disclosed by you or the Company, or the directors, employees or advisers of the Company on a non-confidential basis.

(d) Which was lawfully in our possession prior to such disclosure.

(e) Which is subsequently received by us from a third party without obligations of confidentiality (and, for the avoidance of doubt, we shall not be required to enquire whether there is a duty of confidentiality) or

(f) Which we or a Disclosee are required to disclose, retain or maintain by law or any regulatory or government authority.

3. In consideration of the undertakings given by you in this letter, you agree:

   (a) To disclose Confidential Information to us.

   (b) To keep confidential and not to reveal to any person, firm or company (other than persons within our group who need to know, your bankers and other professional advisers) the fact of our investigation into the Company or that discussions or negotiations are taking place or have taken place.

4. This letter shall be governed by and construed in accordance with English law and the parties irrevocably submit to the non-exclusive jurisdiction of the Courts of England and Wales in respect of any claim, dispute or difference arising out of or in connection with this letter.

5. The undertakings in this letter shall continue to be binding until the earlier of the successful completion of the acquisition of the Company by us, or the date 18 months from the date hereof.

Yours faithfully

APPENDIX 6

Service Agreement

Dated

(1) [COMPANY NAME]

(2) [EMPLOYEE NAME]

SERVICE AGREEMENT

[date]

CONTENTS

THIS AGREEMENT is made the [ ] day of [month] [year]

BETWEEN

(1) **[Company name]** whose registered office is [address] ('the Company')

(2) **[Employee name]** of [address] ('the Executive')

TERMS

1. DEFINITIONS

1.1 In this Agreement the following expressions (whether with or without the definite article) have the following meanings:

'Act'	the Companies Act 1985 (as amended by the Companies Act 1989);
'Agreement'	this agreement;
'Appointment'	the appointment of the Executive, particulars of which are set out in Clause 2;
'Associated Company'	any associated employer, as defined in the Employment Rights Act, of the Company or its holding company or any subsidiary of the Company or its holding company as defined in the Companies Act 1985;
'Board'	the Directors of the Company from time to time present at a meeting of the Directors or of a committee of the Directors duly convened and held;
'Commencement Date'	[date]

'Directors'	the directors of the Company from time to time;
'Employment Act'	the Employment Rights Act 1996;
'Minimum Period'	the period of 18 months from the commencement date set out in Clause 2.2;
'Parties'	the parties to this Agreement.

1.2 Words denoting the singular include the plural and vice versa; and words denoting any gender include both genders.

1.3 References to any statute are to that statute as amended or re-enacted and to any regulation or order made under them.

1.4 References to Clauses and Schedules are to clauses and schedules of this Agreement.

1.5 The Schedules form part of this Agreement for all purposes.

2. THE APPOINTMENT

2.1 The Company shall employ the Executive and the Executive shall serve the Company as Managing Director or in such other capacity as the Company may from time to time direct.

2.2 Subject to the provisions for termination contained in Clauses 8 and 11 of this Agreement, the Appointment shall commence on [date] and shall continue unless and until determined by either party giving to the other not less than six (6) months' notice in writing of such intended determination, such notice to expire at or on any day after the end of the said Minimum Period.

2.3 Notwithstanding any other provision of this Agreement, the Company shall during the period of any notice given pursuant to Clause 2.2 be under no obligation to assign to the Executive any powers or to provide any work for the Executive, and the Company may at any time or from time to time suspend the Executive from the performance of his duties and/or exclude him from the premises of the

Company and require the Executive to stay away from any employees, officers, customers and clients of the Company, but the Executive's salary and other entitlements under this Agreement shall not cease to be payable by reason only of that suspension or exclusion unless this Appointment is subsequently terminated under the provisions of clause 8.

3. DUTIES

3.1   The Executive shall during the Appointment:

3.1.1   devote the whole of his time attention and ability to the duties of his office, and shall diligently perform such duties and exercise such powers as the Board may from time to time properly assign to him in his capacity as Managing Director or in connection with the business of the Company subject to such reasonable directions and restrictions as the Board may from time to time give or impose;

3.1.2   well and faithfully serve the Company and use his best endeavours to promote, develop and extend the business and interests of the Company;

3.1.3   perform such services for Associated Companies and (without further remuneration unless otherwise agreed) accept such offices in such Associated Companies as the Board may from time to time reasonably require;

3.1.4   give to the Board, or such persons as it shall nominate, such information regarding the affairs of the Company as it shall from time to time require;

3.1.5   undertake such travel inside or outside the United Kingdom as may be required for the proper performance of his duties, but he shall not be obliged to reside outside the United Kingdom.

3.2   The Company may from time to time vary the type and nature of the work to be carried out by the Executive and the status and responsibilities connected therewith (provided that his remuneration and benefits are not thereby altered).

3.3 The Executive shall at all times observe and comply with the Company's Rules of Procedure from time to time in force.

3.4 The Company may from time to time appoint any other person or persons to act jointly with the Executive in the Appointment.

3.5 The location at which the Executive shall perform his duties shall be that specified in Clause 15 of Schedule 1.

4. RESTRICTIONS

4.1 The Executive shall not during the Appointment directly or indirectly enter into, or be concerned or interested in, any other trade or business (or occupation) whatsoever which competes with the business of the Company or any Associated Company except with the prior written consent of the Board, but such consent may be given subject to such terms and conditions as the Board may require, any breach of which shall be deemed to be a breach of the terms of this Agreement.

4.2 In this Clause the expression 'occupation' shall include membership of Parliament or of a local authority council or any other public or private work (whether for profit or otherwise) which, in the reasonable opinion of the Company, may hinder or otherwise interfere with the perform ance by the Executive of his duties under this Agreement.

4.3 The Executive shall not without the prior consent of the Board enter into any commitment, contract or arrangement otherwise than in the normal course of business or outside the scope of his normal duties, or of an unusual, onerous or long-term nature.

4.4 The Executive undertakes that he will not during the term of his employment or at any future time use, divulge or disclose to any person, firm or organisation any trade secrets or confidential commercial or technical information relating to the business finances or affairs of the Company. This restriction does not apply to information which is or comes into the public domain otherwise than through unauthorised disclosure by the Executive. Such information will include but shall not be limited to:

4.4.1 the business methods and information of the Company (including but without limitation prices charged, discounts given to customers or obtained from suppliers, product development, marketing and advertising programmes, costings, budgets, turnover, sales targets and other financial information);

4.4.2 lists and particulars of the Company's suppliers and customers and the individual contacts at such suppliers and customers;

4.4.3 details and terms of the Company's agreements with suppliers and customers;

4.4.4 secret manufacturing or production processes and know-how employed by the Company or its suppliers;

4.4.5 confidential details as to the design of the Company's or suppliers' products and inventions or developments relating to future products whether or not in the case of documents they are or were marked as confidential.

These restrictions shall not apply so as to prevent the Executive using his own personal skill in any business in which he may lawfully be engaged after the termination of his employment.

4.5 The Executive shall not during the continuance of this agreement make otherwise than for the benefit of the Company any notes or memoranda relating to any matter within the scope of the business of the Company or of its Associated Companies or concerning any of its or their dealings or affairs, nor shall the Executive either during the continuance of this Agreement or afterwards use or permit to be used any such notes or memoranda otherwise than for the benefit of the Company or of its Associated Companies, it being the intention of the parties hereto that all such notes or memoranda made by the Executive shall be the property of the Company and left at its registered office immediately upon the termination of the Executive's employment hereunder.

5. INVENTIONS ETC.

During the course of his employment the duties of the Executive may result in his making or participating in the making of new and original inventions and implementing improvements by means of such inventions and the creation of plans and documents or other intellectual property. The following subclauses set out the terms and conditions of employment in relation to such matters.

5.1 In these Clauses the expression 'Intellectual Property' shall mean
(a) every invention, discovery, development, process, formula, design, program or improvement (collectively referred to as 'Inventions');
(b) every copyright work or design in which copyright or design rights may subsist and moral rights as defined by the Copyright, Designs and Patents Act 1988 (collectively referred to as 'Works').

5.2 If at any time, during his employment, the Executive makes or discovers or participates with another or any others in making an Invention he must immediately disclose to the Company in confidence full details of any such Invention to allow the Company to determine the ownership of the Invention in accordance with this clause and subject to the Patents Act 1977.

5.3 Inventions made or originated wholly or substantially in the course of the Executive's normal duties or in the course of duties falling outside his normal duties, but specifically assigned to him and where the circumstances in either case were such that Inventions might reasonably be expected to result from his carrying out these duties or in the course of his duties at the time of making the Inventions, and because of the nature of his duties he had a special obligation to further the interest of the Company's undertaking the following subclauses of this Clause shall apply:

5.3.1 Such Inventions (or in the case of Inventions made or originated by him jointly with another or others to the full extent of his interest therein so far as the law allows) shall be held by him in trust for the Company subject to section 39 of the Patents Act 1977, and shall belong to and become the absolute property of the Company and shall not be disclosed to any other person, firm or company without the consent of the Company being previously obtained.

5.3.2 The provisions of this Clause shall not entitle the Executive to any compensation beyond his normal salary. The Company shall only be bound to provide him with additional reward in the case of any Inventions on which a British Patent has been granted or assigned to the Company and in respect of which the Company has derived outstanding benefit from such patent, in which case he may be entitled by virtue of s40 of the Patents Act 1977 to claim additional compensation.

5.3.3 The Executive shall if and when required by the Company and at the expense of the Company provide the Company with all such documents and information and such assistance and do and/or combine with others in doing all acts and sign and execute all applications and other documents (including Powers of Attorney in favour of nominees of the Company) necessary or incidental to applying for obtaining and maintaining or extending patent or other forms of protection for such Inventions in the UK and in any other part of the world or for transferring to or vesting in the Company or its nominees his entire right title and interest to and in such Inventions or to join in any application, patent or other form of protection as the case may be including the right to file applications in the name of the Company or its nominees for patent or other forms of protection in any country claiming priority from the date of filing of any application or other date from which priority may run in any other country.

5.4 If the Inventions are not the property of the Company pursuant to this clause the Company shall, subject to the provisions of s40 of the Patents Act 1977, have the right to acquire for itself or its nominee the Executive's rights in the Inventions and in such circumstances he shall deliver to the Company all documents and other materials relating to the Inventions. The Company shall pay the Executive such compensation as it in its absolute discretion determines fair and reasonable.

5.5 If the Executive creates any Works during his employment then he shall hold them in trust for the Company and all copyright and design rights in such Works shall be the absolute property of the Company in accordance with the Copyright, Designs and Patent Act 1988. The Executive agrees to waive all his rights as granted by Chapter IV of Part 1 of the Copyright, Designs and Patents Act 1988 in respect of any acts of the Company or any acts of third parties done with the Company's authority or in relation to any Works which are the property of the Company by virtue of this Clause, and he shall, at the request and expense of the Company, do all things necessary or desirable to substantiate the rights of the Company under this Clause.

The provisions of this Clause shall remain in force and effect notwithstanding that after the Executive made or originated any such Intellectual Property his employment may have terminated. The provisions of this Clause shall be binding on his representatives.

6. REMUNERATION

6.1 Subject as hereinafter provided, the Company shall pay to the Executive during the continuance of his employment hereunder a salary at the rate of [£amount] per annum or such higher rate as may from time to time be agreed between the parties or determined upon and notified to the Executive by the Company. In the event of any increase of salary being so agreed or notified, such increase shall thereafter have effect as if it were specifically provided for as a term of this agreement. The said salary shall include any sums receivable as director's fees or other remuneration save as provided for in Clause 6.3 hereof. The said salary shall be payable by equal monthly instalments (and proportionately for any lesser period each monthly instalment being deemed to accrue rateably from day to day) in arrears on the last working day of each month.

6.2 Provided the Company is not making losses, on or about each anniversary during the continuance of this agreement the said salary payable under subclause 6.1 of this Clause shall be reviewed by the Board and the rate of salary then payable may be increased by the Board with effect from the date of such review by such amount (if any) as the Board may recommend. The Company shall not be under any obligation to award an increase in the salary.

6.3 Subject as hereinafter provided, the Company shall during the Agreement pay to the Executive as additional remuneration the First Bonus and the Special Bonus (both of which terms are defined in Schedule 2), such bonuses to be calculated and paid in accordance with the terms of Schedule 2.

6.4 The Executive authorises the Company to deduct from the Executive's salary any pay in lieu of notice, any termination payment or any other sums which the Company may owe the Executive, any sums which the Executive may owe the Company, including without limitation any overpayment of salary, bonus or expenses, any debt or loans or any other sum or sums which may be required to be authorised pursuant to section 13 of the Employment Rights Act 1996.

7. BENEFITS

7.1 Car

During such period as the Executive shall be the holder of a valid UK driving licence the Company shall provide and maintain including the costs of taxing and insurance for the sole use of the [type] car or with a car of such make, model, age and specification as is commensurate with his position as an executive of the Company. The Company shall pay for all the running costs, including without limitation maintenance, repairs, oil and petrol.

7.1.1 The Executive shall:

7.1.1.1 comply with all reasonable directions from time to time given by the Company with regard to motor vehicles provided by the Company for the use of its staff;

7.1.1.2 take good care of the car and ensure that the provisions and conditions of any insurance policy relating to it are observed;

7.1.1.3 comply at all times with road-traffic legislation;

7.1.1.4 return the car and its keys to the Company at its registered office (or any other place the Company may reasonably nominate) immediately upon termination of the Appointment (howsoever arising), or at any other reasonable time if so requested for the purpose of inspection.

7.1.2 It is the responsibility of the Executive at the expense of the Company to maintain the car in good running order and in a clean and tidy condition and to keep adequate records in relation to such business use in such form and detail as may be necessary to satisfy any queries in relation to the car which may be raised by HMRC in connection with the Executive's tax affairs, and the Executive is responsible for the payment of any taxes that may be assessed on him for the use of such car. For the purpose of calculating the value to the Executive of the benefit of using the car for his private purposes, the HMRC Scales will be used.

7.1.3 The car shall be replaced from time to time at the Company's absolute discretion and the replacement vehicle shall be commensurate with the Executive's position in the Company.

7.2 Expenses

7.2.1 The Company shall by way of reimbursement pay or procure to be paid to the Executive all reasonable travelling, hotel, telephone, entertainment and other expenses properly incurred by him in or about the performance of his duties under this Agreement subject to the Executive complying with such guidelines or regulations issued by the Company in this respect.

7.2.2 The Executive shall provide reasonable evidence of the expenditure in respect of which he claims reimbursement.

7.2.3 If the Company provides the Executive with a credit or charge card the Executive shall use such card solely for those benefits referred to in Clause 7.2.1. The Executive shall return such card to the Company immediately upon request and in any event on the termination of the Executive's employment.

7.3   Healthcare

7.3.1   The Executive, his spouse and dependent children are entitled to receive the benefit of medical expenses insurance subject always to the terms of such insurance scheme and if and to the extent that such cover is available on normal terms. Full details are available from the Company Secretary.

7.3.2   Any insurance scheme or policy provided to the Executive is subject to the Company's right to alter the cover provided or any term of the Scheme or policy or to cease to provide (without replacement) the scheme or policy at any time if, in the opinion of the Board, the Executive's (or his spouse's or dependant's) state of health is or becomes such that the Company is unable to insure the benefits under the scheme or policy at the normal premiums applicable to a person of the Executive's (or his spouse's or dependant's) age.

7.3.3   The Company shall not have any liability to pay the Executive any benefit under any insurance scheme unless it receives payment from the insurer under the scheme itself.

7.4   Holidays

7.4.1   The Executive shall, in addition to normal bank and public holidays, be entitled to [number] working days' paid holiday in every calendar year, to be taken at such time or times as the Board shall consider most convenient having regard to the requirements of the Company's business. The Executive may not without the consent of the Board carry forward any unused part of his holiday entitlement to a subsequent year.

7.4.2   If the Executive starts or leaves the Appointment during a calendar year, then the Executive's holiday entitlement will be one-twelfth of the holiday entitlement for every completed calendar month of service.

7.4.3   In the event that the Appointment is terminated before the

Executive has taken his holiday entitlement accrued at the date of termination, the Executive shall receive a sum of money equal to his salary for the holiday entitlement accrued but not taken. The entitlement of the Executive to pay in lieu of unused holiday shall be calculated rateably on the basis described in Clause 7.4.2.

7.4.4   The Company may require the Executive to take all or part of any outstanding holiday entitlement during any period of notice to terminate the Executive's employment, including any period of notice during which the Executive is suspended from the performance of all or any of his duties.

8. TERMINATION OF APPOINTMENT

8.1   The Appointment may be terminated by the Company at any time after the Commencement Date immediately without payment of any compensation, redundancy payment, damages or remuneration for subsequent periods payable by virtue of common law or statute, by serving written notice on the Executive in any one or more of the following circumstances if the Executive shall:

8.1.1   be guilty of any gross default or misconduct or wilful neglect in the discharge of his duties under this Agreement;

8.1.2   be guilty of any serious or persistent breach (after warning) or nonobservance of any of the material provisions of this Agreement or directions of the Board;

8.1.3   become bankrupt or make any arrangement or composition with his creditors;

8.1.4   becomes of unsound mind, or becomes a patient for any purpose of any statute relating to mental health;

8.1.5   be convicted of any arrestable criminal offence (other than a motoring offence for which no custodial sentence is made upon him);

8.1.6   carry out any course of action or omission which in the reasonable opinion of the Board may seriously damage the interests of the Company.

8.2   The termination by the Company of the Appointment is without prejudice to any claim which the Company may have for damages arising from breach of this Agreement by the Executive.

8.3   In order to investigate a complaint against the Executive of misconduct, the Company is entitled to suspend the Executive on full pay for so long as may be necessary to carry out a proper investigation.

8.4   Upon the termination of the Appointment for whatever reason, the Executive shall immediately deliver to the Company or to its order all books, documents, papers (including copies), materials, credit cards, keys and other property of or relating to the business of the Company or any Associated Company then in his possession or which are or were last under his power or control.

8.5   In addition to the provisions of this Agreement the Executive shall also comply with such of the Company's disciplinary procedures as are applicable to him.

8.6   The employment of the Executive will terminate automatically on his achieving the normal retirement age of the Company, which is [age] years.

9. EXECUTIVE OBLIGATIONS UPON TERMINATION OF EMPLOYMENT

Upon the termination of his employment hereunder for whatever reason the Executive shall:

9.1   Deliver up to the Company all correspondence, drawings, documents and other papers and all other property belonging to the Company or any Associated Company which may be in the Executive's possession or under his control (including such as may have been made or prepared by or have come into the possession or under the control of the Executive and relating in any way to the business or affairs of the Company or any Associated Company or of any supplier, agent, distributor or customer of the Company or any Associated Company) and the Executive shall not, without the written consent of the Board, retain any copies thereof.

9.2   Not at any time thereafter represent himself as being connected with the Company or any Associated Company.

10. TERMINATION BY RECONSTRUCTION OR AMALGAMATION

10.1   If before the expiration of this Agreement the employment of the Executive hereunder shall be terminated by reason of the liquidation of the Company for the purposes of amalgamation or reconstruction or as part of any arrangement for the amalgamation of the undertaking of the Company not involving liquidation and the Executive shall be offered employment with the amalgamated or reconstructed company on terms not less favourable than the terms of this Agreement, the Executive shall have no claim against the Company in respect of the termination of his employment by the Company.

11. ILLNESS

11.1   If the Executive is absent from work because of illness, mental disorder or injury ('Incapacity'), he must report that fact immediately to the Company Secretary and, after seven continuous days' Incapacity, provide medical practitioners' certificate(s) of his Incapacity and its cause for Statutory Sick Pay purposes covering the whole period of his absence. For Statutory Sick Pay purposes, the Executive's qualifying days are his normal working days.

11.2   If the Executive is absent from work due to Incapacity and has complied with the provisions of Clause 11.1, he will continue to be paid his Salary for a period of one calendar month and then one half of his Salary for a further period of two calendar months provided that any such payment will not be less than and will be deemed to include all and any Statutory Sick Pay to which the Executive is entitled, and any Social Security Sickness Benefit or other state benefits recoverable by him (whether or not recovered) may be deducted from such payment. If the Executive's absence exceeds 30 consecutive calendar days, the Company will be entitled to appoint a temporary replacement to cover his absence.

11.3   The Executive will, whenever requested by the Board, agree to an examination by a medical practitioner selected and paid for by the Company. The Executive hereby authorises such medical practitioner to disclose to and discuss with the Board any matters which, in his opinion, might hinder or prevent him (if during a period of Incapacity) from returning to work for any period or (in other circumstances) from properly performing his duties at any time.

11.4   If the Executive is incapable of performing his duties by reason of circumstances where he has a claim for compensation against a third party and he recovers compensation for loss of earnings whether from that third party or otherwise, he shall repay a sum equal to the amount recovered, or, if less, any amounts paid to him by the Company during his absence.

11.5   Except as expressly provided by this Clause, the Executive shall not be entitled to any salary or bonus in respect of any period during which he shall fail or be unable from any cause to perform all or any of his duties hereunder without prejudice to any right of action accruing or accrued to either party in respect of any breach of this agreement.

12. RESTRICTIVE COVENANTS

12.1   The Executive undertakes that he will not without the prior written consent of the Company (such consent to be withheld only so far as may be reasonably necessary to protect the legitimate interests of the Company or any Associated Company) for a period of twelve months after the termination of this Appointment directly or indirectly on his own behalf or on behalf of any person, firm, or company:

12.1.1   In relation to the provision of any goods or services similar to or competitive with those sold or provided by the Company or an Associated Company at the time of termination and with which he had been concerned or for which he had management responsibilities during the twelve months preceding the termination of this Appointment:

12.1.1.1 solicit or canvass the custom of any person firm or company who at any time during the twelve months prior to the termination of this Appointment was a customer or potential customer of the Company or Associated Company and (in the case of a customer) from whom he had obtained business or to whom he had provided services on behalf of the Company or Associated Company or (in the case of a potential customer) with whom he had dealt with a view to obtaining business for the Company or Associated Company;

12.1.1.2 deal with any person, firm or company who at any time during the twelve months prior to the termination of this Appointment was a customer or potential customer of the Company or Associated Company and (in the case of a customer) from whom he had obtained business or to whom he had provided services on behalf of the Company or Associated Company or (in the case of a potential customer) with whom he had dealt with a view to obtaining business for the Company or Associated Company;

12.1.1.3 employ or offer to employ, or entice away any employee of the Company or Associated Company who was employed by the Company or Associated Company at the time of the termination of this Appointment provided that this restriction shall only apply to persons whom he managed or with whom he had worked at any time during the twelve months preceding the termination of this Appointment and shall not include administrative, clerical, manual and secretarial staff.

12.2 The Executive undertakes that he will not without the prior written consent of the Company (such consent to be withheld only so far as may be reasonably necessary to protect the legitimate interests of the Company or any Associated Company) for a period of twelve months after the termination of his employment directly or indirectly on his own behalf or on behalf of any person, firm or company:

12.2.1 Within a [number]-mile radius of the Company's registered office or of any Associated Company's premises in which he was concerned or for which he had management responsibilities during the twelve months immediately preceding the termination of this Appointment, set up, carry on, be employed in, provide service to, be associated with, or be engaged or interested in, whether as director, employee, principal, agent or otherwise (save as the holder for investment of securities dealt in on a recognised stock exchange) any business which:

12.2.1.1 is or is about to be similar to or competitive with the business carried on by the Company or the Associated Company; or

12.2.1.2 at the date of termination of this Appointment was engaged, interested, or involved in the provision of goods or services similar to or competitive with those sold or provided by the Company or such Associated Company.

12.3 The Executive undertakes that he will not at any time after the termination of this Appointment directly or indirectly on his own behalf or on behalf of a person, firm or company endeavour to impair in any way the relationship between the Company or any Associated Company and any person, firm or company who was at the termination of this Appointment to his knowledge a supplier to or customer of the Company or any Associated Company.

12.4 The restrictions contained in this Clause are considered by the Executive and the Company to be reasonable in all the circumstances. Each subclause constitutes an entirely separate and independent restriction and the duration, extent and application of each of these restrictions is no greater than is necessary for the protection of the interests of the Company or its Associated Companies.

13. POSITIVE WORK ENVIRONMENT

In order that the Company may maintain a positive work environment for all employees, the Executive is required not to engage in or permit any fellow employee to engage in any sexual, racial or other harassment of or unlawful discrimination against any person (whether or not a Company employee) during the Appointment in line with the Company policy on sex and race discrimination from time to time. The Company is an equal-opportunities employer.

14. OTHER AGREEMENTS

The Executive acknowledges and warrants that this Agreement supersedes any earlier agreement as to service and there are no other agreements, whether written, oral or implied, between the Company and the Executive relating to the employment of the Executive other than those set out in this Agreement.

15. GENERAL

15.1 All communications between the Parties with respect to any of the provisions of this Agreement shall be sent to the addresses set out in this Agreement, or to such other addresses as may be notified by the Parties for the purpose of this Clause, by prepaid registered or recorded-delivery post or facsimile transmission or other electronic means of written communication, with confirmation by letter given by the close of business on the next following business day. Any communication to the Company shall be marked 'For the attention of the Company Secretary'.

15.2 Communications which are sent or dispatched as set out below shall be deemed to have been received by the addressee as follows:

by post – two business days after dispatch;

facsimile transmission or other electronic means of written communication – on the business day next following the day on which the communication was sent.

15.3 In proving service by post it shall only be necessary to prove that the communication was contained in an envelope which was duly addressed, stamped and posted by registered or recorded-delivery post. In proving service by facsimile transmission or other electronic means of written communication, proof of service will be accepted on proof of posting of the confirmatory letter.

15.4   For the purpose of Clauses 15.1 and 15.2 a 'business day' means a day on which the clearing banks in the City of London are open for business and 'business hours' means between the hours of 09.00 and 18.00 local time.

15.5   Schedule 1 contains the particulars of the terms of employment of the Executive required by the Employment Act.

15.6   The construction, validity and performance of this Agreement is governed by the laws of England and the Parties agree to submit to the sole and exclusive jurisdiction of the English Courts.

SCHEDULE I

1. **Name of Company**
   [name]

2. **Name of Executive**
   [name]

3. **Period of Employment**
   For the purpose of the Employment Rights Act, the date upon which the Executive's continuous period of service began is [date]

4. **Commencement Date of this Agreement**
   [date]

5. **Position**
   [position]

6. **Notice Period**
   See Clause 2.2

7. **Remuneration**
   See Clause 6

8. **Intervals of Remuneration**
   Monthly

9. **Holidays**

The Executive is, in addition to statutory holidays, entitled to [number] working days' holiday every calendar year and a rateable proportion for a part of a calendar year as calculated in accordance with Clause 7.4, all such days' holiday to be taken at such time or times as shall be convenient to the Company. On the termination of the Appointment, the entitlement of the Executive to holiday pay shall be calculated rateably on the above basis.

10. **Sick Pay**

Subject to Clause 11, there are no terms and conditions relating to incapacity for work due to sickness or injury. Any entitlement to payment during absence from work in other circumstances is at the discretion of the Board.

11. **Pensions**

A contracting-out certificate under the Social Security Pensions Act 1975 is in force in respect of the Appointment. There is a stakeholder pension scheme in which the Executive may participate by virtue of the Appointment. Full particulars will be provided upon application to the Company Secretary.

12. **Grievance Procedure**

The Company's Grievance Procedure will apply to the Executive's employment. A copy of the Procedure is available from the Company's principal place of business.

13. **Disciplinary Procedure**

The Company's Disciplinary Procedure will apply to the Executive's employment. A copy of the Procedure is available from the Company's principal place of business.

14. **Terms and Conditions relating to Hours of Work**

The hours of work of the Executive shall be such hours as may be requisite for the proper discharge of his duties in respect of this Appointment.

The Executive and the Company agree that the limit of an average working time of 48 hours including overtime for each seven-day period as set out in Regulation 4 of the Working Time Regulations 1998 shall not apply to the Executive. This Agreement will remain in force indefinitely unless or until terminated by the Executive at any time by giving not less than three months' written notice to the Company. The Company and the Executive agree that this Agreement complies with the conditions set out in Regulation 5 of the Regulations.

15. **Place of Work**
[Name]

SCHEDULE 2

BONUSES

1. INTERPRETATION

In this Schedule 2 and the Agreement the following expressions shall have the following meanings:

'Adjusted PBT' means (for each Relevant Year and unless already deducted in calculating the PBT) the PBT less:
(1) the First Bonus for that year
(2) any other bonus payable to any other employee of the Company;
(3) (in respect of the relevant Year to [date]) the Deal Costs.

'Deal Costs' means the aggregate amount (excluding VAT) of costs incurred by [Newco] Limited (the parent company of the Company) in connection with the acquisition of the issued share capital of the Company;

'First Bonus' means the bonus payable pursuant to Clause 2;

'Payment Date' means the day which is fourteen days after the date upon which the audited accounts of the Company for the Relevant Year are approved by the shareholders of the Company;

'PBT' means profit before tax of the Company as certified by the Company's accountants for the Relevant Year after making provision for any other bonus payable to any other employee, PROVIDED that in the year to [date] the PBT shall be increased by adding back the Deal Costs;

'Relevant Year'   means [date], [date] or [date] (as the case maybe); and

'Special Bonus'   means the bonus payable pursuant to Clause 3.

2. FIRST BONUS

2.1   The First Bonus shall be payable in respect of each Relevant Year up to and including [date].

2.2   Subject to clause

PBT	First Bonus %
£100,000 or less	2.5%
£100,001 – £250,000	£2,500 plus 7.5% of the amount by which the PBT exceeds £100,000;
£250,001 – £350,000	£13,750 plus 11% of the amount by which the PBT exceeds £250,000;
£350,001 – £450,000	£24,750 plus 14% of the amount by which the PBT exceeds £350,000;
£450,001 – £550,000	£38,750 plus 17% of the amount by which the PBT exceeds £450,000;
£550,001 and above	£55,750 plus 20% of the amount by which the PBT exceeds £550,000.

2.3   The First Bonus is subject to the following conditions:

2.3.1   The First Bonus for each Relevant Year shall not exceed £75,000;

2.3.2   No First Bonus shall be paid unless the Executive is employed by the Company throughout the Relevant Year and the Executive has not on the last day of the Relevant Year given notice to terminate his employment;

2.3.3   In the event that the Executive is dismissed for gross misconduct the Executive shall not be entitled to payment of any accrued or outstanding bonus payment;

2.3.4   After seven months of each Relevant Year the Executive shall be entitled to a payment on account of his prospective entitlement for Bonus, in the sum of 40% of his prospective First Bonus for the Relevant Year based on the management accounts of the Company for the first six months of the Relevant Year PROVIDED that, if such payment on account exceeds the sum payable by way of First Bonus for that Relevant Year, the excess shall be repaid by the Executive within fourteen days of the date upon which his entitlement to First Bonus for that year has been determined and, if not so paid, any such excess may be deducted from any other sums payable to the Executive pursuant to this Agreement.

2.4   Payment of the First Bonus in respect of each Relevant Year shall be made in cash on the Payment Date for that Relevant Year.

2.5   Any bonus which operates from [date] is substituted for the First Bonus, will be entirely at the discretion of the Board of the Company and shall not be a contractual entitlement, unless expressly agreed in writing between the Company and the Executive.

3. SPECIAL BONUS

3.1   The Special Bonus shall be payable in respect of each Relevant Year up to and including [date]. It is not anticipated that any bonus will be provided in substitution for the Special Bonus as from [date].

3.2   Subject to Clause 3.3 Special Bonus shall be calculated as a sum equal to 4% of the Adjusted Profit.

3.3   The Special Bonus is subject to a condition equivalent to that set out in Clause 2.3.2 in respect of the First Bonus (mutatis mutandis);

3.4   The Special Bonus in respect of each Relevant Year shall be paid to the Executive on the Payment Date for that Relevant

Year PROVIDED that the Special Bonus shall be paid by being credited to a loan account in the name of the Executive with [Newco] Limited and shall not be payable by [Newco] Limited to the Executive until the Option Expiry Date (as defined in an Option Agreement to be entered into on the date of this agreement between [Newco] Limited and the Executive).

EXECUTED AS A DEED by the Parties or their duly authorised representatives on the date set out at the head of this Agreement. EXECUTED by

_____

on behalf of [name]

_____

in the presence of:

_____

SIGNED by [name]

_____

in the presence of:

_____

Legal Due-diligence Questionnaire

LEGAL DUE DILIGENCE

INFORMATION REQUEST

CONTENTS

Re: **[Newco] Limited**

References in these enquiries to the 'Company' are to [Newco] Limited and each of its subsidiaries.

Would you please let us have as soon as possible the information and copy documents listed below:

1. **Accounts**
The latest audited accounts of the Company, and if available, draft accounts to [date].

2. **Memorandum and Articles, Resolutions**
The Memorandum and Articles of Association of the Company, together with copies of all Resolutions which need to be filed with the Registrar of Companies.

3. **Charges**
Details of any mortgages, charges or debentures, together with copies of the charging instruments.

4. **Guarantees**
Copies of any guarantees or counter-indemnities given by the Company.

5. **Bank Accounts**
Details of the Company's bank accounts and copies of all facility letters from the Company's bankers.

6. **Consents**
Details of any consents required for the proposed transaction.

7. **Employees**
Copies of all directors' service agreements and full details of all contracts of employment not determinable on [number] month's [or months'] notice or less, a copy of the Company's standard contract of employment for all other employees, together also with details of all bonus or incentive schemes and share options.

8. **Trades Unions**
Details of any agreements with trades unions.

9. **Pensions**
Details of any pension schemes or similar arrangements operated by the Company, with copies of the relevant trust deeds

and rules, employee booklets and notices and the names of the present trustees and actuary.

10. **Intellectual Property**
Details of all trademarks, patents, registered designs, copyright and other industrial property, including any computer software:
10.1 owned by the Company;
10.2 licensed to third parties;
10.3 belonging to others but used by the Company; and
10.4 copies of all relevant agreements.

11. **Litigation**
Short particulars of all pending or threatened claims, litigation, arbitration or similar proceedings (with a note of the amounts involved).

12. **Properties**
12.1 A schedule of leasehold and freehold properties, with brief particulars of each. Please forward copies of the title deeds (including copies of leases granted to the Company as original lessee) and let us know what arrangements can be made for us to examine the deeds. Please also let us have plans of the properties, which will enable us to carry out local searches.
12.2 A list of all licences (governmental or otherwise) required in relation to the operation of the Company's business at the properties.
12.3 Copies of all surveys and reports relating to environmental matters and reports on the impact on the Company's business on the environment, potential health risks at the workplace, the generation and disposal of industrial waste and the compliance of the Company's products with all relevant laws and regulations.

13. **Insurance**
A schedule of current insurance with details as to nature and amount of cover, annual premiums and next renewal date, and details of significant claims made within the last 12 months.

14. **Agreements**
Full details of:
14.1 Any agreements or arrangements currently in operation

which are liable to termination or alteration on the sale of the Company;

14.2 Full particulars of any services provided by the sellers, the amounts currently payable for such services and whether the sellers envisage any transitional arrangements;

14.3 Details of any transactions between the Company and the sellers or any of the directors or any companies connected with any of them;

14.4 Details of all hire-purchase, rental, leasing and similar agreements, with copies to be made available in due course;

14.5 Details of any long-term or unusual agreements, including all joint-venture agreements;

14.6 Details of outstanding capital commitments;

14.7 Copies of all agency and distribution agreements; and

14.8 Details of any foreign-exchange exposure of the Company and of the Company's policy concerning forward transactions in foreign exchange.

15. **Shareholders**
A full list of present shareholders with details of their holdings of [each class of] shares. Where shares are held in nominee names or by trustees, please clarify the beneficial ownership of the shares.

16. **Officers**
A list of the present directors and the secretary, together with particulars as to their responsibilities and their remuneration.

17. **Tax**
Details of the Company's tax position – to what date are its corporation tax returns agreed? To what date have shortfall clearances been applied for and obtained? Are there any tax matters outstanding or in dispute? Is the Company a close company? Copies of tax computations for the last three years are required. Are there tax losses available for carrying forward?

18. **Subsidiaries**
A list of the Company's subsidiaries and Subsidiary undertakings (if any). We require particulars of all the matters listed above in relation to each subsidiary and subsidiary undertakings.

Sample Shareholders' Agreement

Dated   2005

[Name 1]

– and –

[Name 2]

– and –

[Name 3]

– and –

[Name 4]

– and –

[Name 5]

– and –

[NEWCO] LIMITED

SUBSCRIPTION AND SHAREHOLDERS' AGREEMENT

relating to

[company]

SUBSCRIPTION AND SHAREHOLDERS' AGREEMENT

Date: [date]

Parties:

(1)   [**Name 1**] of [**address**] ('N1');

(2)   [**Name 2**] of [**address**] ('N2');

(3)   [**Name 3**] of [**address**] ('N3');

(4)   [**Name 4**] of [**address**] ('N4');

(5)   [**Name 5**] of [**address**] ('N5');

(6)   [**Newco**] **LIMITED** (registered in England with company number [number]) whose registered office is situated at [address] (the '**Company**')

RECITALS:

(A) The Company was incorporated under the Companies Act 1985 on [date] with company number [number] and at the date of this Agreement has an authorised share capital of £[sum] divided into [number] 'A' Ordinary Shares and [number] 'B' Ordinary Shares.

(B) N1 is the sole shareholder in the Company and this Agreement has been entered into to document an allotment of 'A' Ordinary Shares to N1, N2 and N3 and the allotment of the 'B' Ordinary Shares to N4 and N5 pursuant to the Share Purchase Agreement and to regulate the relationship between the Directors and the Shareholders in connection with the management and finances of the Company.

OPERATIVE PROVISIONS:

1. INTERPRETATION

1.1   In this Agreement:

'**A**' **Ordinary Shareholders** means N1, N2 and N3, being the holders of the 'A' Ordinary Shares or any person or persons to whom they may properly transfer their 'A' Ordinary Shares pursuant to the provisions of this Agreement;

'A' Ordinary Shares means the 'A' Ordinary Shares of £1 nominal value in the capital of the Company;

Agreed Terms means in the form of a document agreed between the Parties;

Agreement means this Agreement;

Articles means the articles of association (and memorandum of association) of the Company;

'B' Ordinary Shareholders means N4 and N5, being the holders of the 'B' Ordinary Shares or any person or persons to whom they may properly transfer their 'B' Ordinary Shares pursuant to the provisions of this Agreement;

'B' Ordinary Shares means the 'B' Ordinary Shares of £1 nominal value in the capital of the Company to be allotted to N4 and N5 on Completion in accordance with the Share Purchase Agreement;

Board means the board of Directors for the time being of the Company;

Business means the business of the Company as described in Clause 3.1 and such other business as the Parties may agree from time to time in writing should be carried on by the Company;

Business Day means 9.00am to 5.00pm on any day (other than a Saturday or Sunday) on which clearing banks in the City of London are open for the transaction of normal Sterling banking business;

Chairman means any chairman appointed by the Board or Shareholders pursuant to the Articles;

Change of Control means the acquisition by any person of any interest in any Shares if, upon completion of that acquisition such person, together with persons acting in concert or connected with them, would hold more than 50% of the Shares;

Completion means completion of this Agreement in accordance with Clause 2;

Connected Party means

(a) in relation to an individual:

(i) that individual's spouse, children, stepchildren and grandchildren (together 'the individual's family') and the trustees (acting as such) of any trust of which the individual or any of the individual's family is a beneficiary or discretionary object (other than a trust which is either an occupational pension scheme (as defined in section 1 of the Pension Schemes Act 1993) or an employees' share scheme (as defined in section 743 of the Companies Act) which does not, in either case, have the effect of conferring benefits on persons all or most of whom are themselves Associates);

(ii) any company in whose equity shares the individual and/or members of the individual's family (taken together) are directly or indirectly interested (or have a conditional or contingent entitlement to become interested) so that they are (or would on the fulfilment of the condition or the occurrence of the contingency be) able to:

(A) exercise or control the exercise of 30% or more of the votes able to be cast at general meetings on all, or substantially all, matters; or

(B) appoint or remove directors holding a majority of voting rights at board meetings on all, or substantially all, matters; and

(b) in relation to a company:

(i) any other company which is its subsidiary undertaking or parent undertaking or a subsidiary undertaking of the parent undertaking (as those expressions are defined in section 258 of the Act);

(ii) any company whose directors are accustomed to act in accordance with its directions or instructions; and any company in the capital of which it and any other company under paragraph (b) (i) or (b) (ii) above taken together is (or would on the fulfilment of a condition or the occurrence of a contingency be) interested in the manner described in paragraph (a) (ii) (B) above;

Director means any director for the time being of the Company including where applicable any alternate director appointed in accordance with the Articles;

Equity Share Capital shall have the meaning ascribed to such expression by section 744 of the Companies Act 1985;

Independent Accountant means an independent accountant appointed jointly by the Parties or in the absence of agreement appointed at the request of either Party by the President for the time being of the Institute of Chartered Accountants of England and Wales;

Parties means the parties to this Agreement and Party shall be construed accordingly;

Shareholders means the 'A' Ordinary Shareholders and the 'B' Ordinary Shareholders;

Share Purchase Agreement means of today's date a share purchase agreement relating to the purchase of the entire issued share capital of [Company Name] by the Company to be made between [Owner] (1) N4 (2) N5 (3) and the Company (4);

Shares means the 'A' Ordinary Shares and the 'B' Ordinary Shares; and

Subsidiary and **Holding Company** shall have the meanings ascribed to such expressions by section 736 of the Companies Act 1985.

1.2   Any reference to a statute, statutory provision or subordinate legislation shall be construed as referring to that statute, statutory provision or subordinate legislation as amended, modified, consolidated, re-enacted or replaced and in force from time to time, whether before or after the date of this agreement (but not where to do so shall have the effect of expanding or increasing any Warranty or other liability), and shall also be construed as referring to any previous statute, statutory provision or subordinate legislation amended, modified, consolidated, re-enacted or replaced by such statute, statutory provision or subordinate legislation.

1.3 Any reference to a statutory provision shall be construed as including references to all statutory instruments, orders, regulations or other subordinate legislation made pursuant to that statutory provision.

1.4 Unless the context otherwise requires:

1.4.1 words denoting the singular include the plural and vice versa;

1.4.2 words denoting any gender include genders;

1.4.3 a reference to a 'company' includes any company, corporation or other body corporate, wherever in the world and however that company was incorporated or established; and

1.4.4 a reference to a 'person' includes any individual, firm, company, government, state or agency of a state or any joint venture, association or partnership (whether or not having separate legal personality).

1.5 Clause headings are for convenience only and shall not affect the interpretation or construction of this Agreement. Any reference to a clause, subclause, paragraph or schedule is to the relevant clause, subclause, paragraph or schedule of this agreement.

1.6 The Recitals and Schedules to this Agreement shall for all purposes form part of this Agreement.

1.7 Any phrase introduced by the terms 'including', 'include', 'in particular' or any similar expression shall be construed as illustrative and shall not limit the sense of the words preceding those terms.

1.8 Except as otherwise expressly stated in this Agreement, all representations, warranties, undertakings, agreements, covenants, indemnities and obligations made or given or entered into by Parties under this Agreement are assumed by them jointly and severally.

2. COMPLETION

2.1 Completion will take place immediately following the signing of this Agreement at such time, date or place as the Parties may agree.

2.2 On Completion:

2.2.1 the Company shall allot and issue the following 'A' Ordinary Shares to N1, N2 and N3 (subject to the Company receiving the required funds):

(1)	(2) 'A' Ordinary Shares	(3) Subscription monies (£)
N1	* * * * *	* * * * *
N2	* * * * *	* * * * *
N3	* * * * *	* * * * *

2.2.2 the Company shall register N1, N2 and N3 as the holders of the 'A' Ordinary Shares set out opposite their respective names in column 2 of subclause 2.2.1 and shall prepare and deliver share certificates in respect of such 'A' Ordinary Shares.

2.2.3 the Company shall allot and issue the following 'B' Ordinary Shares:

(1)	(2) 'B' Ordinary Shares	(3) Investment monies (£)
N4	* * * * *	* * * * *
N5	* * * * *	* * * * *

2.2.4 the Company shall register N4 and N5 as the holders of the 'B' Ordinary Shares set out opposite their respective names in column 2 of subclause 2.2.3 and shall prepare and deliver share certificates in respect of such 'B' Ordinary Shares.

3. OBJECTS OF THE COMPANY

3.1 The primary object of the Company shall be to carry on the business of [business].

3.2 The Business shall be conducted in the best interests of the Company on sound commercial profit-making principles so as to generate the maximum achievable maintainable profits available for distribution.

4. APPOINTMENT OF DIRECTORS

4.1 At the date of this Agreement the sole Director is N1.

4.2 On Completion:

4.2.1 N2 and N3 shall be appointed as Directors; and

4.2.2 N1 shall be appointed as Chairman of the Board and shall remain as Chairman unless and until the Directors unanimously resolve otherwise in accordance with subclause [   ].

4.3 In the case of an equality of votes at any meeting of the Board the Chairman shall [not] be entitled to a second or casting vote.

4.4 The number of Directors holding office at any time shall not be subject to any maximum unless otherwise expressly agreed in writing by each of the Shareholders and the minimum shall be three.

4.5 In consideration of the provisions relating to dividends and distributions set out in article [number] of the Articles, the total monetary remuneration excluding taxation (PAYE and national insurance contributions (both employees' and employer's contributions)), private medical insurance, life assurance, company car benefits (if any), pension contributions (both employees' and employer's contributions), plus any further exclusions, of all of the Directors holding 'A' Ordinary Shares (in their capacity as employees of the Company), shall not exceed the gross sum of £ [sum] unless otherwise agreed in writing by all of the Shareholders.

5. CONDUCT OF THE COMPANY'S AFFAIRS

5.1 The Shareholders shall exercise all voting rights and other powers of control available to them in relation to the Company so as to procure (insofar as they are able by the exercise of such rights and powers) that at all times during the term of this Agreement, unless otherwise agreed in writing by all of the Shareholders:

5.1.1 The business of the Company consists exclusively of the Business;

5.1.2 The Shareholders shall each be entitled to examine the separate books and accounts to be kept by the Company and to be supplied with all relative information, including monthly management accounts and operating statistics and such other trading and financial information, in such form as they may reasonably require to keep each of them properly informed about the Business, the Company and any Subsidiary of the Company and generally to protect their interests;

5.1.3 The auditors of the Company shall be such firm of chartered accountants and registered auditors as the Shareholders may agree should be appointed;

5.1.4 The bankers of the Company shall be the [name of bank] or such other bank appointed by the Directors;

5.1.5 The registered office of the Company shall be located at [address] or at such other place as the Shareholders may approve;

5.1.6 All cheques of the Company up to the value of £[sum] shall be required to be signed by any one Director;

5.1.7 All cheques of the Company in excess of £[sum] shall be required to be signed by two Directors;

5.1.8 The Company shall comply with the provisions of its Articles;

5.1.9 The Articles shall not be altered and no further articles or resolutions inconsistent therewith shall be adopted or passed unless the terms of the Articles or resolutions have been previously approved in writing by each of the Shareholders;

5.1.10 The Company shall procure that any company which becomes a Subsidiary of the Company at any time during the term of this Agreement shall adopt new articles of association in a form approved by the Shareholders.

5.2 Board meetings shall be convened, at regular intervals not exceeding [time] by not less than [time] notice in writing to the Directors accompanied by an agenda specifying the business to be transacted.

5.3 In order to transact any business at a Board meeting a quorum must be present. For the purposes of this Agreement a quorum shall consist of at least [number] Directors personally present or subject to Clause 5.4 by alternate at a duly convened meeting of the Board.

5.4 If any Director shall be unable to attend a Board meeting for any reason whatsoever he shall be entitled to nominate such person as he thinks fit to attend such Board meeting in his place and to vote on any issue arising. The instrument appointing such substitute Board member shall be in writing and shall be produced to the other Board members on or before such meeting. If a Director appoints another Director as his alternate, the appointee shall have the right to a vote on behalf of his appointor as well as his own vote.

5.5 Minutes of all Board meetings shall be distributed to the Directors and their alternates.

5.6 In circumstances where a resolution of the Board is required this may be achieved without calling a meeting of the Board in accordance with Clause 5.2, provided that a written resolution to that effect is signed by all the Directors entitled to attend and vote at such meetings.

5.7 The Board by majority vote will determine the general policy of the Company and of any Subsidiary (subject to the express provisions of this Agreement), including the scope of their respective activities and operations and the Board will reserve to itself [(for unanimous decision or 50% as the case may be)] all matters which in the reasonable opinion of the Board constitute major or unusual decisions including:

5.7.1 borrowing any money in excess of any limits between the Shareholders, or creating any mortgage, debenture, pledge, lien or other encumbrances over the undertaking or assets of the Company, or factoring, assigning, discounting or otherwise disposing of any book debts or other debts of the Company requiring [unanimous decision/a 50% vote];

5.7.2 making any loan or advance or giving any credit in excess of £[sum] to any person, except for the purpose of making deposits with bankers, which shall be repayable upon the giving of no more than seven days' notice; requiring [unanimous decision/a 50% vote];

5.7.3 giving any guarantee or indemnity to secure the liabilities or obligations of any person, requiring [unanimous decision/a 50% vote];

5.7.4 the selling, transferring, leasing, assigning, or otherwise disposing of a material part of the undertaking, property and/or assets of the Company (or any interest therein), or contract so to do; requiring [unanimous decision/a 50% vote];

5.7.5 the entering into of any contract, arrangement or commitment involving expenditure on capital account or the realisation of capital assets if the amount or the aggregate amount of such expenditure or realisation by the Company, and all (if any) of the Subsidiaries of the Company would exceed £[sum] in any one year, or in relation to any one project, and for the purpose of this subclause the aggregate amount payable under any agreement for hire, hire purchase or purchase on credit sale or conditional sale terms shall be deemed to be capital expenditure incurred in the year in which such agreement is entered into; requiring [unanimous decision/a 50% vote];

5.7.6 engaging any new employee of the Company at remuneration which could exceed the rate of [   ] per annum, requiring [unanimous decision/a 50% vote];

5.7.7 increasing the remuneration of any Director or employee of the Company to a rate which could exceed the rate of [   ] per annum, requiring [unanimous decision/a 50% vote];

5.7.8 taking or agreeing to any leasehold interest in or licence over any land; requiring [unanimous decision/a 50% vote];

5.7.9 creating, acquiring or disposing of any branches of the Company or any Subsidiary or of any shares in any Subsidiary, requiring [unanimous decision/a 50% vote];

5.7.10 entering into any partnership or profit-sharing agreement with any person; requiring [unanimous decision/a 75% majority];

5.7.11 entering into any contract or transaction (except in the ordinary and proper course of the Business on arm's-length terms); requiring [unanimous decision/a 50% vote];

5.7.12 agreeing and changing any dividend policy of the Company requiring [unanimous decision/a 50% vote];

5.7.13 recommending to the Shareholders any dividend or other distribution requiring [unanimous decision/a 50% vote];

5.7.14 changing the structure and organisation of the Company; requiring [unanimous decision/a 50% vote];

5.7.15 recommending to the Shareholders an increase in the authorised share capital of the Company; requiring [unanimous decision/a 50% vote];

5.7.16 agreeing and approving corporate planning and strategy of the Company; requiring [unanimous decision/a 50% vote];

5.7.17 determining terms of employment of the Company's employees; requiring [unanimous decision/a 50% vote];

5.7.18 recommending to the Shareholders approval of the annual financial statements and reports; requiring [unanimous decision/a 50% vote];

5.7.19 approving the taking or defending legal or arbitration proceedings; requiring [unanimous decision/a 50% vote];

5.7.20 agreeing financial matters regarding bank arrangements of the Company (including the giving of any guarantees, indemnities or security); requiring [unanimous decision/a 50% vote];

5.7.21 employing and dismissing senior employees of the Company; requiring [unanimous decision/a 50% vote];

5.7.22 agreeing and approving financial policies in relation to the profit and financial conditions of contracts of the Company; requiring [unanimous decision/a 50% vote];

The indication '50%' or 'unanimous' in the above subclauses indicates the level of voting required.

6. MATTERS REQUIRING CONSENT OF ALL SHAREHOLDERS

The Shareholders shall exercise all voting rights and other powers of control available to them in relation to the Company so as to procure (insofar as they are able by the exercise of such rights and powers) that neither the Company nor any Subsidiary of the Company shall without the prior written consent of all Shareholders:

6.1 issue any unissued share for the time being or create or issue any new shares, except as expressly permitted by the Articles;

6.2 alter any rights attaching to any class of Share;

6.3 consolidate, subdivide or convert any of the Shares;

6.4 issue renounceable allotment letters or permit any person entitled to receive an allotment of Shares to nominate another person to receive such allotment except on terms that no such renunciation or nomination shall be registered unless the renunciation or person nominated is approved by the Board; or

6.5 do or permit or suffer to be done any act or thing whereby the Company may be wound up (whether voluntarily or compulsorily), save as otherwise expressly provided for in this Agreement;

6.6 create any contract or obligation to pay money or money's worth to any Shareholder or to any person as a nominee or associate of any such Shareholder (including any renewal thereof or any variation in the terms of any existing contract or obligation);

6.7 hold any meeting of Shareholders or purport to transact any business at any such meeting unless there shall be present duly authorised representatives, alternatives or proxies for each of the Shareholders respectively; or

6.8 the sale or disposal of any property and/or assets of the Company (or any interest therein) with a market value in excess of [£ sum].

7. FINANCE

The Directors shall each use reasonable endeavours to procure that the requirements of the Company for working capital to finance the Business are met as far as is practicable by borrowings from banks and other financial institutions on the most favourable terms reasonably obtainable as to interest, repayment and security, but without allowing any prospective lender a right to participate in the Equity Share Capital of the Company and its Subsidiaries as a condition of any loan.

8. GUARANTEES AND INDEMNITIES

8.1 The Shareholders agree that, subject to subclauses 8.2 and 8.3 the aggregate amount of any actual liability incurred by them pursuant to any joint-and-several guarantee or indemnity given by them to any third party in respect of any liabilities or obligations of the Company and/or its Subsidiaries or pursuant to any guarantee or indemnity (whether several or joint-and-several) given in respect of such obligations or liabilities by any of them with the written consent of the others shall be borne by them equally and each shall indemnify and keep indemnified the others accordingly.

8.2 If any liability incurred under subclause 8.1 is solely attributable to the act or default of one Shareholder then, notwithstanding subclause 8.1, the whole of such liability shall be borne by such Shareholder, who shall indemnify and keep indemnified the other Shareholders accordingly.

8.3 In the event that any Shareholder disposes of all his or its Shares to any of the other Shareholders then the Shareholders acquiring such Shares will use all reasonable endeavours to obtain the release of that Shareholder from any guarantees and indemnities which he may have given pursuant to this Agreement or with the written consent of the other Shareholders in respect of any of the liabilities or obligations of the Company and its Subsidiaries to third parties and pending the obtaining of such release shall keep that Shareholder fully and effectually indemnified against any liability pursuant to any such guarantees or indemnities.

9. CHARGING OF THE SHARES

None of the Shareholders shall, except with the prior written consent of the other Shareholders, create or permit to subsist any pledge, lien or charge over, or grant any option or other rights or dispose of any interest in, all or any of the Shares held by him or it (otherwise than by a transfer of such Shares in accordance with the provisions of this Agreement) and any person in whose favour any such pledge, lien or charge is created or permitted to subsist or such option or rights are granted or such interest is disposed of shall be subject to and bound by the same limitations and provisions as embodied in this Agreement.

10. TRANSFERS

10.1   The Directors will not register a transfer of any Share unless the transfer is permitted by Clause 10.3 or has been made in accordance with Clause 11.

10.2   Where any Shares are the subject of a Transfer Notice (defined under Clause 11) no transfers of any Shares shall be permitted pursuant to Clause 10.3.

10.3   Subject to Clause 10.2 above, any Shares may be transferred pursuant to Clause 12 (Compulsory Transfer), Clause 13 (Drag-along) or Clause 14 (Tag-along).

11. TRANSFER OF SHARES

11.1   Except in the case of a transfer pursuant to Clause 12 (Compulsory Transfer), Clause 13 (Drag-along) or Clause 14

(Tag-along), a Shareholder who wishes to transfer any Shares is required to do so according to the following provisions.

11.2   Any Shareholder who wishes to transfer Shares or any interest in Shares (other than as provided in Clauses 11.14 and 11.1.5 below) (the Vendor) shall give to the Company notice in writing (the Transfer Notice). A Transfer Notice shall constitute the Directors as the Vendor's agents for the sale of the Shares specified in it (the Sale Shares) at a price (the Sale Price) which is agreed upon by the Vendor and the Directors or, in the absence of agreement, which bears the same proportion as the nominal value of the Sale Shares does to the nominal value of the whole of the issued share capital of the Company to the price which the Independent Accountant (acting as an expert and not as an arbitrator) certifies to be in his opinion the fair value of the whole of the issued share capital of the Company, as at the date of the Transfer Notice, as between a willing seller and a willing buyer contracting on arm's-length terms, having regard to the fair value of the business of the Company and its Subsidiaries (if any) as a going concern and such other matters as may, in their reasonable opinion, be relevant at that time.

11.3   Within five Business Days of the issue of the Independent Accountant's certificate the Directors will send a copy to the Vendor. The cost of obtaining the certificate shall be borne by the Vendor and the certificate shall be binding upon all Parties. A Transfer Notice shall not be revocable without the consent of all the Directors, who may impose such condition upon any consent as they think fit, including a condition that the Vendor bears all associated costs.

11.4   Upon the Sale Price being agreed or certified, the Directors shall promptly, by notice in writing, offer the Sale Shares:

11.4.1 in the case of 'A' Ordinary Shares, to all 'A' Ordinary Shareholders (other than the Vendor) pro rata as nearly as may be to the respective numbers of 'A' Ordinary Shares held by such 'A' Ordinary Shareholders; and

11.4.2   in the case of 'B' Ordinary Shares, to all 'A' Ordinary Share-holders (other than the Vendor) pro rata as nearly as may be to the respective numbers of 'A' Ordinary Shares held by such 'A' Ordinary Shareholders.

11.5   Any offer made by the Directors under Clause 11.4 will invite the 'A' Ordinary Shareholders to state in writing the maximum number of Sale Shares they wish to purchase and any additional Sale Shares they wish to purchase if these are not taken up by the other 'A' Ordinary Shareholders. This offer will remain open for [   ] Business Days (the First Offer Period).

11.6   If at the end of the First Offer Period there are any Sale Shares offered which have not been allocated as a result of some or all of the 'A' Ordinary Shareholders not taking the number of Sale Shares offered to them pursuant to Clause 11.4, the Directors shall promptly offer the remaining Sale Shares to all of the Shareholders pro rata as nearly as may be to the respective numbers of Shares held by the Shareholders.

11.7   Any offer made by the Directors under Clause 11.6 will invite the Shareholders to state in writing the maximum number of Sale Shares they wish to purchase. If there are insufficient remaining Sale Shares to meet the demand then the Directors will allocate the remaining Sale Shares pro rata as nearly as may be in proportion to the number of Shares held by the Shareholders wishing to purchase additional Sale Shares. This further period will remain open for a fur-ther period of [   ] Business Days (the Second Offer Period).

11.8   For the purpose of this clause, the First Offer Period and the Second Offer Period shall be known collectively as the Acceptance Periods.

11.9   If within the Acceptance Periods the 'A' Ordinary Share-holders or the Shareholders (as applicable) (the Transferees) accept any offer for all or any of the Sale Shares, the Direc-tors shall promptly give notice in writing (the Acceptance Notice) to the Vendor specifying the number of Sale Shares taken up and the place and time (being not earlier than [   ] and not later than [ ] Business Days after the date of the Acceptance Notice) at which the sale shall be completed.

11.10   The Vendor shall be bound to transfer the Sale Shares, or such of the Sale Shares as are applied for, to the Transferees at the time and place specified in the Acceptance Notice and payment of the Sale Price for the Sale Shares (or, if some only of the Sale Shares have been applied for, the corresponding proportion of the Sale Price for all the Sale Shares) shall be made to the Directors as agents for the Vendor. If the Vendor fails to transfer the Sale Shares, or such of the Sale Shares as are applied for, the Chairman or some other person appointed by the Directors shall be deemed to have been appointed attorney of the Vendor with full power to execute, complete and deliver, in the name and on behalf of the Vendor, transfers of the Sale Shares, or such of the Sale Shares as are applied for, to the Transferees against payment of the Sale Price, or the corresponding proportion of the Sale Price, to the Company. On payment to the Company, the Transferees shall be deemed to have obtained a good discharge for this payment. On execution and delivery of the transfers, the Transferees shall be entitled to require their names to be entered in the register of members as the holders by transfer of the Sale Shares or such of the Sale Shares as are applied for. The Company shall pay the price into a separate bank account in the Company's name and hold it in trust for the Vendor, after deducting any fees or expenses falling to be borne by the Vendor. After the names of the Transferees have been entered in the register of members in purported exercise of the above powers, the validity of the proceedings shall not he questioned by any person.

11.11   If, following the Acceptance Periods, not all of the Sale Shares have been taken up, then the Directors may, in their absolute discretion, notify, the Vendor in writing within ten Business Days after the expiry of the Second Offer Period of their intention to procure the Company to repurchase all of the remaining Sale Shares (but not some of them), and shall simultaneously convene an extraordinary general meeting of the Company to consider a resolution to approve such a repurchase. If no such notice is given by the Directors, or if notice is given but the necessary shareholders' resolution is not passed at the first attempt, or if the resolution is passed but the repurchase is not completed within ten Business Days thereafter, then the Vendor shall be at liberty during the period of six months following the expiry of the Second Offer Period to transfer all or any of the remaining Sale Shares to any person at a price not being less than a due proportion of the Sale Price. The Directors may require to be satisfied that the Sale Shares not taken up are being transferred in pursuance of a bona fide sale for the consideration stated in the transfer without any deduction, rebate or allowance of any kind to the purchaser and, if not satisfied, may refuse to register the instrument of transfer. A Director who is, or is nominated by, the Vendor shall not be entitled to vote at any board meeting at which a resolution to the sale is proposed.

11.12 Upon transferring any of the Sale Shares to the Transferees or to a third party in accordance with the provisions of this clause the Vendor shall procure that all Directors appointed by him to the Board resign and, pending registration of the transfer, shall assist (if necessary) in procuring that Directors nominated by the Transferee or such third party are appointed in their place.

11.13 Notwithstanding the above, the Directors may decline to register a transfer of a share on which the Company has a lien.

11.14 The restrictions on transfer contained in this Clause shall not apply to a transfer approved in writing by all the Shareholders.

12. COMPULSORY TRANSFER

12.1 The provisions of this Clause 12 shall apply to:

12.1.1 a Shareholder holding Shares who is an individual and not a corporate body and ceases to be an employee and/or Director, a director any of its Subsidiaries or is declared bankrupt; and

12.1.2 a Shareholder who is a corporate body and not an individual and suffers any insolvency event (including, but not limited to, the inability to pay its debts as they fall due, entry into administration, receivership, administrative receivership or liquidation (either compulsory or voluntary, except for the purposes of amalgamation or reconstruction) the passing of a resolution for a creditors winding up, the making of a proposal to its creditors for a composition in satisfaction of its debts or a scheme of arrangement of its affairs, the application to the court for an administration order and the appointment of an administrative receiver and in relation to the various insolvency events they are, wherever appropriate, to be interpreted in accordance and conjunction with the relevant provisions of the Insolvency Act 1986 (as amended by the Enterprise Act 2002) (Insolvency Event).

12.2   For the purposes of this Clause such a Shareholder who is an individual shall be deemed to be a Good Leaver if he:

12.2.1   dies;

12.2.2   suffers serious illness or serious disablement; or

12.2.3   retires at or after the normal retirement age of 65; or

12.2.4   is dismissed other than as mentioned in Clause 12.3.2; or

12.2.5   is declared bankrupt; or

12.2.6   resigns as a Director.

12.3   For the purposes of this Clause a Shareholder who is an individual who:

12.3.1   is not a Good Leaver; or

12.3.2   is dismissed for gross misconduct shall be deemed to be a Bad Leaver.

12.4   For the purposes of this Clause a Shareholder who is a corporate body and suffers any Insolvency Event shall be deemed to be a Good Leaver.

12.5   A Shareholder shall be deemed to have served a Transfer Notice in respect of all the Shares registered in his name upon the date of the event specified in Clauses 12.2 to 12.4

(inclusive) or, if later, the date when the Directors became aware of such event.

12.6 The provisions of Clauses 11.1 to 11.12 (inclusive) shall apply to any such Transfer Notice, provided that for these purposes:

12.6.1 the Sale Shares shall comprise all of the above-mentioned Shares; and

12.6.2 the Sale Price shall be determined by Clause 12.7;

12.7 The Sale Price shall be:

12.7.1 in the case of a Good Leaver, the Fair Price (determined in accordance with Clause 12.8); or

12.7.2 in the case of a Bad Leaver, the par value of the Sale Shares.

12.8 The Fair Price shall be such price as the Shareholder and the Company shall agree within ten Business Days of the date of the deemed Transfer Notice or failing such agreement such price as the Independent Accountant shall determine pursuant to Clause 11.2.

13. DRAG-ALONG

13.1 In this Agreement a Qualifying Offer shall mean an offer in writing by or on behalf of any person, being a bona fide third party who, for the avoidance of doubt, is not a Connected Party (Offeror) to all of the holders of Shares to acquire all their Shares which:

13.1.1 is stipulated to be open for acceptance for at least fifteen Business Days;

13.1.2 offers the same consideration for each Share;

13.1.3 includes an undertaking by or on behalf of the Offeror that no other consideration (whether in cash or otherwise) is to be received or receivable by any Shareholder which, having regard to the substance of the transaction as a whole, can reasonably be regarded as an addition to the price paid or payable for the Shares to be sold by such Shareholder, and that neither the Offeror nor any person acting by agreement or understanding with it has otherwise entered into more favourable terms or has agreed more favourable terms with any other Shareholder for the purchase of the Shares;

13.1.4 is on terms that the sale and purchase of the Shares in respect of which the offer is accepted will be completed at the same time.

13.2 If a majority in number of the Shareholders (the Accepting Shareholders) wish to accept the Qualifying Offer, then the provisions of this clause shall apply.

13.3 The Accepting Shareholders shall give written notice to the remaining Shareholders (the Other Shareholders) of their wish to accept the Qualifying Offer. The Other Shareholders shall thereupon become bound to accept the Qualifying Offer and transfer their Shares to the Offeror (or his nominee) with full title guarantee on the date specified by the Accepting Shareholders.

13.4 If any Other Shareholders shall not, within five Business Days of being required to do so, execute and deliver transfers in respect of the Shares held by them and deliver the certificate(s) in respect of the same (or a suitable indemnity in lieu thereof), then any Accepting Shareholders shall be entitled:

13.4.1 to transfer their Shares directly to the Offeror and Clause 11 shall not apply to such transfer(s); and

13.4.2 to execute, or authorise and instruct such person as he thinks fit to execute, the necessary transfer(s) and indemnities on the Other Shareholders' behalf; and

13.4.3 against receipt by the Company (on trust for such Other Shareholders) of the consideration payable for the Shares, to deliver such transfer(s) and indemnities and share certificate in respect of the Shares to the Offeror (or his nominee) and to register such Offeror (or his nominee) as the holder thereof and the validity of such proceedings shall not be questioned by any person.

14. TAG-ALONG

14.1   If at any time one or more of the Shareholders (Proposed Sellers) propose to sell, in one or a series of related transactions, a majority in nominal value of the Shares (Majority Holding) to any person being a bona fide third party and who, for the avoidance of doubt, is not a Connected Party and not being an Offeror for the purposes of Clause 13.1, the Proposed Sellers may only sell the Majority Holding if they comply with the provisions of this clause.

14.2   The Proposed Sellers shall give written notice (Proposed Sale Notice) to the other remaining Shareholders of such intended sale at least ten Business Days prior to the date thereof. The Proposed Sale Notice shall set out, to the extent not described in any accompanying documents, the identity of the proposed buyer (Proposed Buyer), the purchase price and other terms and conditions of payment, the proposed date of sale (Proposed Sale Date) and the number of Shares proposed to be purchased by the Proposed Buyer (Proposed Sale Shares).

14.3   Any Shareholder (Remaining Shareholder) shall be entitled, by written notice given to the Proposed Sellers within ten Business Days of receipt of the Proposed Sale Notice, to be permitted to sell, and the Proposed Buyer shall be required to buy for the same consideration for each Share as the Proposed Buyer is paying to the Proposed Sellers all of the Remaining Shareholder's Shares on the same terms and conditions as the Proposed Buyer is offering.

14.4   If any other Shareholders are not given the rights accorded him by the provisions of this clause, the Proposed Sellers shall be required not to complete their sale and the Company shall be bound to refuse to register any transfer intended to carry such a sale into effect.

15. EXERCISE OF VOTING RIGHTS

Each Shareholder undertakes with the other(s) as follows:

15.1   to exercise all voting rights and powers of control available to him in relation to the Company so as to give full effect to the terms and conditions of this Agreement including, where appropriate, the carrying into effect of such terms as if they were embodied in the Articles;

15.2   generally to use his best endeavours to promote the Business and the interests of the Company.

16. THIS AGREEMENT NOT TO CONSTITUTE A PARTNERSHIP

None of the provisions of this Agreement shall be deemed to constitute a partnership between the Shareholders and none of them shall have any authority to bind the other in any way.

17. COSTS

All costs, legal fees and other expenses incurred in the preparation and execution of this Agreement shall be borne and paid by the Company.

18. NONDISCLOSURE OF INFORMATION

None of the Shareholders shall divulge or communicate to any person (other than whose province it is to know the same or with proper authority) or use or exploit for any purpose whatever any of the trade secrets or confidential knowledge or information or any financial or trading information relating to the other Shareholders and/or the Company which the relevant Shareholder may receive or obtain as a result of entering into this Agreement, and shall use its reasonable endeavours to prevent its employees from so acting. This restriction shall continue to apply after the expiration or sooner termination of this Agreement without limit in point of time but shall cease to apply to information or knowledge which may properly come into the public domain through no fault of the Shareholder so restricted.

19. DURATION

This Agreement shall continue in full force and effect until the first to occur of the following dates:

19.1   The date on which a Change of Control occurs; or

19.2   The date of commencement of the Company's winding up

provided that the terms of this Agreement shall nevertheless continue to bind the Shareholders thereafter to such extent and for so long as may be necessary to give effect to the rights and obligations embodied in this Agreement.

20. ASSIGNMENT

None of the Shareholders shall assign or transfer or purport to assign or transfer any of his rights or obligations hereunder without the prior written consent of the other Shareholders and the assignor guaranteeing by deed the due performance of the assignee's obligations in accordance with the provisions of Clause 23.

21. SUCCESSORS AND ASSIGNS

This Agreement shall endure for the benefit of and be binding on the respective successors in title and permitted assigns of each Shareholder who shall procure in transferring any of their Shares in the Company that each such transferee shall execute a deed with the other Shareholders by which the transferee agrees to be bound by terms identical, mutatis mutandis, to the terms of this Agreement (including the terms of this Clause as regards any subsequent transfer of the Shares).

22. WAIVER, FORBEARANCE AND VARIATION

22.1   The rights of either party shall not be prejudiced or restricted by any indulgence or forbearance extended to the other party and no waiver by any party in respect of any breach shall operate as a waiver in respect of any subsequent breach.

22.1   This Agreement shall not be varied or cancelled, unless such variation or cancellation shall be expressly agreed in writing by the Parties to this Agreement.

23. SEVERABILITY

If any of the provisions of this Agreement is found by a court or other competent authority to be void or unenforceable, such provision shall be deemed to be deleted from this Agreement and the remaining provisions of this Agreement shall continue in full force and effect. Notwithstanding the foregoing the Shareholders shall thereupon negotiate in good faith in order to agree the terms of a mutually satisfactory provision to be substituted for the provision so found to be void or unenforceable.

24. THE TERMS OF THIS AGREEMENT TO PREVAIL

In the event of any ambiguity or conflict arising between the terms of this Agreement and those of the Articles, the terms of this Agreement shall prevail as between the Shareholders.

25. NOTICES

25.1 Any notice to be given under this Agreement shall either be delivered personally or sent by first-class recorded-delivery post (airmail if overseas). The address for service of each Shareholder shall (in the case of a company) be its registered office for the time being and (in the case of an individual) shall be his address stated above or any other address for service previously notified to the other Shareholder or (in the absence of any such notification) his last known place of residence. A notice shall be deemed to have been served as follows:

25.1.1 if personally delivered, at the time of delivery; and

25.1.2 if posted, at the expiration of forty-eight hours or (in the case of airmail) seven days after the envelope containing the same was delivered into the custody of the postal authorities.

25.2 In proving such service it shall be sufficient to prove that personal delivery was made, or that the envelope containing such notice was properly addressed and delivered into the custody office of the postal authority as a prepaid first-class recorded-delivery or airmail letter (as appropriate).

26. GENERAL MATTERS

26.1 This Agreement supersedes any previous agreement between the Parties in relation to the matters dealt with herein and represents the entire understanding between the Parties in relation thereto.

26.2 Reference to any statute or statutory provision includes a reference to that statute or statutory provision as from time to time amended, extended or re-enacted.

26.3 Words denoting the singular number only shall include the plural and vice versa.

26.4 Unless the context otherwise requires, reference to any clause or schedule is to a clause or schedule of or to this Agreement.

26.5 The headings in this Agreement are inserted for convenience only and shall not affect the construction hereof.

27. GOVERNING LAW

27.1 The construction, validity and performance of this Agreement shall be governed in all respects by English law.

27.2 The High Court of England shall have jurisdiction to settle any dispute which may arise between the Parties in respect of the construction validity or performance of this Agreement or as to the rights and liabilities of the Shareholders hereunder or in any way connected with the Company and the Shareholders hereby agree that in the event of any action in respect of this Agreement being begun the process by which it is begun may be served on them in accordance with the provision of Clause 25.

IN WITNESS whereof this agreement was executed as a deed and delivered the day and year first above written

SIGNED as a Deed and Delivered by N1 in the presence of:

Witness Signature _____

Name _____

Address _____

_____

Occupation _____

SIGNED as a Deed and Delivered by N2 in the presence of:

Witness Signature _____

Name _____

Address _____

_____

Occupation _____

SIGNED as a Deed and Delivered by N3 in the presence of:

Witness Signature _____

Name _____

Address _____

_____

Occupation _____

SIGNED as a Deed and Delivered by N4 in the presence of:

Witness Signature _____

Name _____

Address _____

_____

Occupation _____

SIGNED as a Deed and Delivered by N5 in the presence of:

Witness Signature _____

Name _____

Address _____

_____

Occupation _____

EXECUTED as a Deed and Delivered by [   ]

LIMITED acting by _____

and)

Director _____

Director/Secretary _____

APPENDIX 9

Financier's Due-diligence Questionnaire

Financial due-diligence summary

Section: History and Nature of Business
Client:
Assignment:

Objective: To describe the history and recent development of the business, its overall structure and mode of operation.

It is not possible to provide a definitive checklist for this section. Set out below is a summary of those areas that will most commonly be included in this section.

Done n/a

1. Provide brief overview of the history of the business, including date incorporated, summary of activities, geographical locations and branch structure, share and ownership structure.

2. Provide analysis and commentary on major products in terms of sales and profitability, together with a description of different sales methods. This would also include an assessment of what is happening to the company's market share, product range and product age.

3. Review the markets in which the company operates together with a summary of relevant market research into recent and anticipated developments.

4. Summarise and review the target's strategy.

5. Review sales to major customers with commentary on reasons for any changes over the period (particularly lost customers) together with details of any contractual relationships.

6. Comment on overall pricing policy with details of any major discounts offered.

7. Describe the main terms of trade, highlighting in particular any contingent sales, sale-or-return agreements, retrospective agreements etc.

8. Analyse the sales and marketing functions together with details of main promotional activities and the extent to which these functions interact with other elements of the business.

9. Summarise methods of distribution together with a summary of any distribution agreements.

10. Review the principal suppliers with commentary on any changes over the period and a commentary of the products and services supplied. Provide details of any reliance on individual suppliers.

11. Summarise any supply agreements with particular note as to any exclusive licensing or distribution agreements.

12. An overview, if relevant, of the development and production function with details of any unique technologies, patents or other intellectual property rights together with a summary of how these are protected.

13. Details of major competitors with an analysis, if possible, of management's view of the target's strengths and weaknesses.

14. Exposure to risks, e.g. exchange rate, political, customer or supplier.

Section: Management and Personnel

Client:

Assignment:

Objective: To provide details of management, key personnel and the organisational structure of the company, together with an assessment thereof.

Done n/a

1. Assess the adequacy of management, and identify personnel essential to the ongoing prosperity of the business.

2. Consider the overall organisational structure of the company, and identify significant weaknesses or inefficiencies.

3. Identify unusual features, such as compensation payment clauses, labour or skill shortages, management succession problems etc.

4. Are there any apparent deficiencies in the abilities of management?

5. Are any personnel of such importance that the loss of their services would be detrimental to the performance of the business?

6. Is there a clear delineation of duties with responsibility for the major roles appropriately distributed, e.g.

   - managing director;
   - sales/marketing directors;
   - product director;
   - finance director?

7. Is the overall organisational structure appropriate to the business?

8. Is there any unusual or excessive remuneration?

9. Do labour-force difficulties exist, such as supply problems, union difficulties and high staff turnover?

10. Will changes in labour legislation have a major impact on the business, e.g. minimum wage, Working Time Directive etc.?

11. Are staff subject to ongoing training?

12. Does the company have difficulty recruiting appropriate staff?

13. Summarise terms and conditions of employment of key directors and staff.

14. Summarise terms and conditions as they apply to the remainder of the staff.

Section: Accounting Systems and Controls

Client:

Assignment:

Objective: To provide general details of the accounting systems and level of internal control, identify key weaknesses and comment on internal reporting procedures.

Done n/a

1. Document the company's accounting systems and if necessary evaluate the impact of any weaknesses upon the reliability of the financial statements.

2. Are the personnel in charge of the accounting system suitably qualified, skilled and experienced?

3. Is there sufficient accounting resource and is the segregation of duties appropriate to the size and nature of the business (cash-based transactions will normally require a greater degree of segregation of duty).

4. Are the accounting system and accounting resource sufficient to meet the requirements of any planned expansion in the business?

5. Are management accounts prepared and are they:

   prepared on a regular and timely basis;

   sufficiently detailed compared to the nature of the business;

   accompanied by a commentary against previous years/budget;

   accurate (by reference to adjustments to derive audited financial information)?

6. Are budgets prepared and are appropriate staff involved in the process (including approval)?

7. Are budgets prepared in sufficient detail, including balance sheet and cash flows? Are the profit and loss, cash flow and balance sheet integrated?

8. Are budgets updated during the year to take account of changing circumstances?

9. Have previous budgets been accurate compared to actual historical results (where we are reviewing projections)?

Section: Accounting Policies

Client:

Assignment:

Objective: To summarise the accounting policies of the company, and to comment upon their appropriateness and compatibility with those of the acquiring company.

Done n/a

1. Summarise the significant accounting policies as they appear in the last audited accounts and summarise the detailed ways they are applied in practice. ☐☐

2. Comment on the accounting policies, where appropriate, in terms of compliance with UK GAAP, our client's policies and industry standards. ☐☐

3. Have the target's accounting policies changed in the period under review? ☐☐

4. Does the company apply the same accounting policies as the acquirer and, if not, what is the impact on the historical trading results and balance sheet of restating using the acquirer's policies? ☐☐

5. Are there any areas subject to particularly high levels of judgement by the directors? ☐☐

6. Does the company have any ongoing contingent liabilities in respect of its major products, e.g. sale-or-return agreements, retrospective discounts, and, if so, are they properly accounted for? ☐☐

7. What is the policy for recognising income (this is not usually explicitly stated)? ☐☐

Section: Historical and Current Trading

Client:

Assignment:

Objective: To provide a summary of trading results for the period under review, together with suitable analyses of figures contained therein, and a commentary explaining the trading results of individual periods and the trend thereof.

These are normally two separate sections. However, their content will typically be similar with the current trading review building on the knowledge obtained during the review of historical trading

Done n/a

1. Are changes in the level of activity and profitability over the period adequately explained?

2. Are changes in sales and the product mix explained and are any trends apparent? Can changes in the level of activity be analysed between volume and price factors?

3. Is the company dependent on a small number of products for the majority of its sales?

4. Are new products being introduced (including in the current period) to replace sales of ageing products?

5. What are the principal components of direct costs? Is there a substantial proportion of fixed cost and what are the implications of this for any changes in the level of activity?

6. Have movements in direct costs been influenced by material changes in supplier prices over the period?

7. Is gross margin broken down on a product-by-product basis and are any movements adequately explained? What are the ongoing implications of any continued movements in gross margin?

8. Are the major elements of overheads explained together with any underlying reasons for changes in the level of costs? In particular:

   staff costs;

   sales and marketing costs;

   distribution costs;

   premises costs;

   repairs and maintenance expenditure;

   legal and professional fees.

Is the level of costs appropriate for the business, e.g. high
proprietor expenses may be charged? Are intercompany charges
supportable by reference to services received and what are the
implications of any changes in ownership, e.g. lower/higher
on-going costs?

9. Are any private expenses charged through the profit and loss
account?

10. Have we identified and commented on any exceptional
charges/credits over the period or other nonrecurring
expenditure?

11. Has any expenditure of a capital nature been written off
through the profit-and-loss account, e.g. major development or
refurbishment costs?

12. For the current trading period, compare actual results with the
current budget and the corresponding period in the previous
year.

13. Where we have not carried out a review of the history and
nature of the business, consider whether the following should
be included under historical trading:

    - analysis of major customers;
    - analysis of major suppliers;
    - reliance on particular contracts;
    - reliance on other group companies.

Section: Historical Cash Flow

Client:

Assignment:

Objective: To provide a summary of historical cash flows for the period
under review, together with an analysis of the seasonality of cash/
borrowing requirements

Done n/a

1. Set out the historical cash flows and comment on major cash
flows under the principal headings, particularly those relating to
movements in working capital.

2. Highlight the effect of nonoperating cash flows, particularly those of a nonrecurring nature, e.g. major capital additions, purchase or sale of businesses, share issues, repayment of loans.

3. Analyse monthly balances over a period and, if possible, comment on periods of peak borrowing to the extent that there is any seasonality in cash flow.

Section: Review of Projected Trading

Client:

Assignment:

Objective: To provide a summary of projected trading results and a commentary upon the reasonableness thereof.

Done n/a

1. Summarise the projected trading results, comparing them with the last completed period of trading.

2. If appropriate, divide the current year into the actual results for the period to date and the projected results for the remainder of the period.

3. Have any changes in the projected levels of activity and profitability of the company been adequately explained in the light of both historical and current financial performance?

4 Set out the key assumptions used in preparing the projections and comment on the reasonableness thereof in the light of recent experience and external factors (e.g. inflation).

5. What is the basis of preparation of the projections (e.g. part of normal budgetary routine) and have appropriate personnel been involved?

6. Establish whether the projected results have been prepared on a 'top down' (e.g. sales will grow by 10% next year) or a 'bottom up' basis (e.g. sales to individual customers or by individual product lines have been estimated). The latter should provide more comfort to us.

7. How accurate have previous budgets been (see also Accounting Systems and Controls)?

8. Are the projections subject to key uncertainties, e.g. the introduction of new products, changes in pricing, securing major new contracts or renegotiating existing contracts, significant reduction in costs?

9. Comment on projected sales, including monthly sales, product mix, pricing, and note whether the projections are consistent with recent trends.

10. Can significant changes in the projected level of sales be explained by reference to new products, product relaunches etc., and are these supportable by reference to the development of the product and previous product launches/relaunches?

11. What are the major components of direct costs and are the levels of costs and gross margins consistent with recent experience and historical and current trends?

12. To what extent are direct costs and overheads variable and are the projected costs consistent with both historical and current experience and projected changes in the levels of activity?

13. If a reduction in the projected level of activity is anticipated, has provision been made for related costs, e.g. redundancy, losses on disposal of assets?

14. If activity is projected to expand, are current premises adequate?

NB: This programme is to be used in the performance of a limited review of forecast trading, e.g. when we are requested to comment upon the projected results of an accounting period for which management accounts are available for at least the first half of that accounting period. This programme assumes that current trading has already been reviewed. In all instances where either a detailed review of projected trading is requested, or public comfort is to be given by the due-diligence team upon a profit forecast, reference must be made to Section 4 of the Corporate Finance Directions manual, and the work programmes contained therein must be utilised.

Section: Review of Balance Sheet/Net Assets
Client:
Assignment:

Objective: To provide a summary of the balance sheet and appropriate analyses of figures contained therein, and to comment upon the nature and validity of assets and liabilities.

Done n/a

1. Intangible assets

Where intangible assets (including development costs) are included on the balance sheet, have we considered the basis for their inclusion and commented on any uncertainties surrounding their realisation?

Have we adequately explained the valuation basis and the amortisation period?

2. Fixed assets

Summarise and comment on the major components on fixed assets.

Does the company have any specialist fixed assets which may be difficult to replace or, if a reduction in the level of activity is anticipated, to dispose of?

Discuss the basis of valuation and compare carrying values to any recent external valuations.

Comment on security over fixed assets, e.g. asset registers and physical verifications.

Are the depreciation rates and bases appropriate?

In the case of production-based companies, are assets subject to an ongoing renewal programme?

Are any provisions in respect of lease dilapidations necessary?

3. Stocks and work in progress ('WIP')

Summarise stock and WIP.

Are movements in the overall levels of stocks and WIP consistent with the trading activities of the business?

Have stocks and WIP been analysed by type and by products? If so, are the levels of each stock line consistent with the level of sales in the most recent period under review?

Summarise the basis of valuation of stock and WIP. In particular, where direct and overhead costs are absorbed, are the costs appropriate and are the absorption rates consistently applied year on year?

Have the auditors attended stocktakes and verified the existence of stocks and WIP?

How often does management carry out stocktakes and are these full or partial?

Are perpetual stock records maintained and, if so, how accurate are these?

Are any stock-ageing reports available and, if so, what do they indicate re the need for any stock provision?

How are price and obsolescence provisions calculated and are the movements in the provisions consistent with movements in stock levels and the level of activity?

4. Trade debtors

Are the levels of trade debtors consistent with the levels of activity over the period?

Are debtor days consistent over the period with any material fluctuations explained, and what do they indicate re standard trading terms?

Summarise standard trading terms.

Are trade debtors aged and does this indicate any substantial older balances?

Is the analysis of debtors consistent with the analysis of major customers?

Have material balances been repaid since the end of the period and, if not, why? Do the directors have any significant concern re the recoverability of major balances?

What is the basis for the bad-debt provision and is it consistent with the level of activity and the age profile of debts?

Is there a credit-note provision and what is its basis?

5. Other debtors and prepayments

Is the level of other debtors and prepayments consistent over the period? If not, explain major movements.

Comment on material balances.

6. Intercompany balances

How are intercompany balances to be treated following the proposed acquisition and have we commented on the implications of this?

7. Cash overdrafts and loans

Summarise cash overdraft and loan balances. What are the principal terms of loans and overdraft facilities. Will these require repayment in the near future?

Are there any onerous terms in the overdraft and loan agreements and have we provided a summary of the major covenants (if applicable)?

8. Trade creditors

Is the level of trade creditors consistent with level of activities? Are major fluctuations in the levels of creditors explained?

Summarise the terms of trade with suppliers.

Are creditors aged and, if so, does the profile suggest that payments have been delayed?

Are the major trade creditors consistent with the analysis of major suppliers?

9. Accruals and other creditors

Are the levels of accruals other creditors consistent with the level of activity?

Comment on major balances and major movements in balances.

Do taxation creditors reconcile to supporting data, e.g. payroll, VAT returns and corporation tax returns?

10. Provisions

Are provisions analysed by type, including deferred tax? Have there been any material movements in provisions over the period and are any movements supported by underlying documentation?

Do discussions with directors and a review of other documents suggest that any further provisions may be necessary or that there are contingent liabilities in respect of other matters?

Is there a material unprovided deferred tax asset or liability?

Is the pension scheme fully funded and, if not, how has the surplus or deficit been treated and what are the ongoing cash and profit-and-loss implications of this?

11. Share capital and reserves (to be completed only in the case of a share acquisition)

Summarise the rights of each class of different type of share. Are the abilities to take trading, financing and dividend decisions restricted by the existence of minorities? Do minorities have rights to appoint directors?

Are there any undistributable reserves?

Section: Taxation

Client:

Assignment:

Objective: To summarise the current status of corporation tax, PAYE and VAT affairs, identify problems and disputes and consider the tax implications of the proposed transaction.

Done n/a

Corporation tax

1. Have tax liabilities/losses been agreed in respect of the period for which the last audited accounts have been made up and, if

not, does a review of the computation suggest that there may be material amounts subject to dispute?

2. Has deferred taxation been provided for correctly and are there material unprovided assets or liabilities?

3. Has ACT been accounted for correctly?

4. What are the major tax implications of the structure proposed for the transaction?

5. Have appropriate tax warranties been obtained in the purchase contract?

6. Have we commented on the proposed structure of the transaction and considered the tax implications of this for the acquirer and considered the existence of more efficient alternative structures?

Payroll taxes

7. Has a detailed PAYE review been carried out and does this indicate the existence of material potential unprovided liabilities? These will normally arise from benefits and other matters not accounted for via the payroll system.

VAT

8. Has a detailed VAT review been carried out and does this indicate the existence of material potential unprovided liabilities?

9. Have we considered the VAT implications of the transaction and considered the existence of more efficient alternative structures?

Section: Other Matters

Client:

Assignment:

Objective: To provide details of and comment on any matters of significance not covered by other sections of our report

Done n/a

1. Summarise details of insurances (including cover for disruption of trade and computer breakdown).

2. What is the nature of any pension scheme and, in the case of a
defined benefit scheme, is it fully funded? ☐☐

3. Is the pension scheme compatible with that of the acquirer? ☐☐

4. What is the effect of profit-sharing schemes on retained
earnings? ☐☐

5. Have we summarised the principal terms of leases and do
property-rental agreements contain onerous clauses, e.g. regular
refurbishment costs, rent reviews or service charges? ☐☐

6. Where the company has substantial operating leases, are there
potential commitments where usage exceeds that agreed in the
lease, e.g. excess mileage costs or additional copy costs? Are the
minimum agreed usages appropriate for the activities of the
business? ☐☐

7. Is there a possibility of material costs or losses being incurred in
respect of outstanding legal actions? ☐☐

8. Have material capital commitments been entered into? ☐☐

9. What are the principal terms of major dealership/agency
agreements, e.g. minimum purchase values or quotas, rebate
/discount levels, territory, cancellation? ☐☐

10. Are statutory books and registers properly maintained? ☐☐

11. Are there unusual clauses or restrictions in the Memorandum
and Articles of Association? ☐☐

Index